Yes Miss Hardy

An entertaining and heart-warming memoir
of becoming a primary school teacher

AMELIA HARDY

Mereo Books

2nd Floor, 6-8 Dyer Street, Cirencester, Gloucestershire, GL7 2PF
An imprint of Memoirs Books. www.mereobooks.com
and www.memoirsbooks.co.uk

Title of Book: Yes Miss Hardy
ISBN: 978-1-86151-972-6

First published in Great Britain in 2020
by Mereo Books, an imprint of Memoirs Books.

The address for Memoirs Books can be
found at www.mereobooks.com

Mereo Books Ltd. Reg. No. 12157152

Typeset in 11/15pt Century Schoolbook
by Wiltshire Associates.
Printed and bound in Great Britain

'To write is to save things from vanishing for ever.'
Annie Ernaux

In memory of my mother
16.9.1917 – 10.8.2015

While this memoir is based on real characters and events, the names, details and timings may have been changed to aid the narration.

Acknowledgements

I would like to thank my family and friends who have given me their support and encouragement while I have been writing this memoir, not forgetting my husband, who has ensured the manuscript was not deleted by the press of a button.

FOREWORD

~~~~~

Thoughts from 'Alison', a good friend who shared part of this particular journey.

Memories, expectations and first impressions of life as young student teachers… a tiny slice of social history. We went into this new stage of our young lives with hope, excitement and not a little apprehension of what lay ahead, a blank page waiting to be filled with new adventures. These experiences and escapades certainly made for a colourful and rewarding three years for us all, as budding teachers in the late sixties and early seventies. It was an unknown journey which was supported by great friendships and a growing independence. The world of primary education was opening out before us…

CONTENTS

~~~

CHAPTER ONE

~~~

MAY 1969

THE START OF SOMETHING NEW

"Tell me, why do you want to teach?"

I look blankly across the desk at the tutor. She stares back at me through horn-rimmed spectacles. A clock on the wall ticks away the seconds slowly and loudly. Is there no air in this room? I need to breathe.

This is the big question I've been waiting for during my interview for a place at a teacher training college. I'm ready for this. For weeks now, I've thought about it, prepared and rehearsed at home: in the bedroom, in the bathroom, in the kitchen. One answer I am determined not to give, with an adorable expression on my face, is, 'because I love children'. Too predictable. Who can love all children? My sister has told me all about whining Wayne in her Reception Class.

I press dry lips together and resist the urge to adjust the collar of my new white blouse. I'm hoping the embroidered flowers are showing above the neckline of my equally new cardigan in royal blue. I'm still not convinced that the colour matches my navy pleated skirt, which is my 'Sunday best'.

I twist my fingers on my lap. The tutor clears her throat. Still waiting.

At last my practised reply comes to me. It tumbles out all in one breath.

"Well, I want to pass on all the benefits of my own education and my experience to young children." Just for good measure, I add, "And to make them aware of the wonderful world around them".

The only thing I am aware of at this very moment is how I must look the complete opposite of someone with experience. But the tutor rewards me with a half-smile and my shoulders relax. It's much easier now to give an account of my weekly Sunday School class, the kind of books I like to read, the classics, of course, and my years of practice on the piano. All of which I am hoping will add to the picture of me as a potential teacher.

It feels like an hour, but is really only a few gruelling minutes later, when I skip out of that stuffy room. My mother's voice is ringing in my ear, 'Just try your best'. It is her daily mantra and I know that's all she expects of me and I've done just that.

I think I'm falling in love with College: the long, echoing corridors, the smell of polished floors, the high ceilings and the grand main staircase. And the warmth. Warmer than my school or the draughty house at home.

I slow down and start to take small, measured steps, determined to remember all the details. This original part of the building, so I have been told, houses the offices and the libraries. I can hear typewriters clacking and a low murmur of voices behind closed doors.

Behind one of them, apparently, is Miss Pringle's room. She is the Principal and, I gather, much respected. Further along the corridor, I find her portrait on the wall. Sitting bolt upright, she certainly looks impressive and not a little imposing, with silvery, white hair scraped back from her face and a stern but not severe gaze. I detect a hint of kindness there. Or at least I'd like to think so. The tutor who has just interviewed me said that should I be offered a place, I would get to meet Miss Pringle. She made it sound like a great privilege.

Reluctantly, I leave by the main door, hearing it thud behind me. Lingering for a while under a canopy of stone arches, I feel awkward in my interview attire. Around me, students, mainly dressed in jeans and baggy T-shirts, wander here and there in groups of twos and fours, arms full of files, intent on their destinations of lectures or perhaps back to Halls of Residence. They are all talking, laughing, their faces bright and animated and I long to be one of them.

Aware that my mother is waiting for me and keeping calm by drinking tea in a little café down in town, I head up the long sweep of the drive. When I reach the grand wrought iron gates leading to the main road, I turn left and walk along the pavement by a low wall which skirts the grounds and the vast, neat lawns, fringed by tall sycamore and horse chestnut trees.

Now I can see the full effect of the college buildings, so elegant with an imposing entrance and long Victorian windows. There's a heady smell of newly cut grass and a continual cooing sound from wood pigeons, soft and rhythmical. I stand on the pavement under the trees, surveying the scene, unwilling to leave.

It's here: that's what I've been talking about to the tutor in the overly heated interview room. I thought my vision of a wonderful world was full of blues and greys, reflected in the sea from the sky. I thought it was the drama of stormy waves, wind-lashed onto the pier and the outline of a black pit wheel turning. But now, in front of me, are shades of greenery and the shapes of trees. The air is full of bird song and the horizon a strip of blue, which isn't the coast as it would be at home, but a line of far-away hills. As I feel the stirrings of the lure of the countryside, I know that this is the right place for me to embark on the journey from pupil to teacher, from child to adult.

It's as if my future is laid out before me. I see myself swishing through the fallen leaves in autumn, perhaps picking up a few colourful ones to use later; I might even stand too long to watch a squirrel up in the branches on my way to lectures. This day is only the beginning, the start of something new.

Well, I must have said the right thing weeks ago on that interview day, because this morning, an acceptance letter fell onto the front door mat. It states in black and white that a place is being offered to me at St Margaret's Church of England College of Education in North Yorkshire. I've read it a dozen times to make myself believe it. My mother and sister are full of wide smiles and congratulations. I am quietly ecstatic.

So, I am going to teach.

No, I wasn't always going to. The fact that Judith, my elder sister by seven years, is a teacher made the whole idea seem repugnant, at first.

"What are you going to do when you grow up, Amelia? Be a teacher?" Usually this would come from a lady from church, towering over me, with a head of tightly permed curls. Very rudely I would curl my lip and say with a scowl that I was going to be an airline pilot or an actress to shock and appal that well-meaning person.

Besides which, my mother was convinced that, unlike my sister, I didn't have the temperament. When we were little, if we played schools, she always had to be the teacher. I was the one who stayed in the background, drawing pictures on the backs of old birthday cards or making up stories in an empty exercise book.

By the age of fourteen, so adamant was I that I would not take up the chalk and duster that my good sister, during her first year of teaching, and probationary at that, invited me into her lively, boisterous Reception Class. To experience 'a day in the life of' you might say. Not to hurt her feelings, I accepted.

Thirty-odd four to five-year-olds from a deprived council estate in a mining town might daunt the most courageous. Quivering heart I may have, but a stout exterior has always won me through. 'Very confident manner', my elocution teacher would often remark, when inwardly I was quaking in my black patent leathers.

Well, back to 'a day in the life of'. By playtime I was involved, by dinner time I was enthralled, but come home time, I was hooked. There was nothing tangible to help explain the attraction: simply the atmosphere of friendly helpfulness, the general hubbub and the organised chaos in that infant classroom proved irresistible.

As an onlooker, the whole process looked as easy as passing the time of day. But, as my sister assured me, put yourself in front of the blackboard, or behind the desk with a register, or in the middle of children, painting, glueing and cutting, and the game can slip away from you, as if you've forgotten the rules and your class, loyal two minutes ago, has just invented a whole new set. Judith said that despite three years of training, you only really learn the hard way when to be pleased and when to act annoyed. According to her it was an act, a performance, if you will.

In the classroom that day, I watched my sister hold up flash cards of Peter and Jane, guide the first squiggles of a fat pencil and encourage colourful marks with a paintbrush. I could see myself in the teacher's chair, or rather shoes. Judith said the only time she sat down was at the end of the day when the children had gone home.

It's September now. My last week of freedom, or limbo between school and College is passing in a flurry of buying everything I might need, from a tin opener to toothpaste and teabags. Trying to fit them all into a large second-hand trunk is proving to be more difficult than I imagined. A long list of essentials sent from College includes a dictionary and the complete works of Shakespeare, as my main subject is to be English. A list of non-essentials but things I want to take with me consists of: a thick green St Margaret's College scarf with cream stripes (which I am determined to wear constantly) and a matching green blazer complete with embroidered badge (which I'm not so sure about). Both paid for by my kind grandmother.

Money is tight in my family, as my mother has been a widow since just after my birth. She has to account for every penny spent, so we beg and borrow as much as we can. On the 'Preferable but Non-Essential' list is a rug to act as a bedspread. One of my favourite aunties has bought me a tartan one which looks very cheerful, mainly in red. That too is stuffed into the trunk, along with all my clothes and shoes, not forgetting a regulation PE kit.

Many an evening this summer has been spent talking to my mother and sister in the kitchen, the place where all the important discussions and events have taken place throughout my life. It was the kitchen where at the tender age of five, I had sat on my little wooden stool and cried after I'd careered down the front street on Judith's Tri-ang scooter and then flown head over heels across the handlebars. It was in the kitchen where at the age of twelve or thirteen I would stare into the flames of the coal fire, wrestling with the realisation that I was leaving childhood behind and wondering whether there was some possible way I could halt the process. Persisting in wearing white ankle socks and having my hair in plaits hadn't seemed to make much difference: my body changed into womanhood without any consent from me.

And in this very same kitchen, unchanged with its green and white gas cooker standing in the corner and the table with a checked cloth under the window, the three of us have talked and talked: about how leaving home is an adventure, how I will discover a world beyond the red brick terraces, the yards and back streets. I've glimpsed that vision of greenery already.

It's not only my familiar home town I will be leaving but my family of mother, sister, grandmother and a long line of aunties, all loving and caring, strong and dependable. Until my eighteenth birthday, just this summer, I have been 'the baby', the one to be looked after. Soon I will have only myself to rely upon.

Who are the new people I will have to live with, and more importantly, am I fit for the challenge?

CHAPTER TWO

~~~

SEPTEMBER 1969

TOUGH LOVE

The strains of Glenn Miller's 'In the Mood' fill the corridor. An unlikely choice of music, I think, and pop my head out of the door to see where it's coming from.

"Hope you don't mind." A girl appears from the doorway of the furthest room. "It's my Granddad's favourite and I'm hooked on it now."

She leans in a casual way against the door frame, one hand in the pocket of flared patched jeans. Her fair hair hangs long and loose, parted like curtains on either side of an angular face. Stepping forward, she introduces herself in a strong, Yorkshire accent as Penny from Leeds.

As my room-mate hasn't yet arrived, I'm relieved to take a break from unpacking to meet my next-door neighbour. Penny shows me her turntable with the old seventy-eight record spinning round on it, churning out Glenn Miller's tunes. It's my first introduction to 'Pennsylvania 6 5 0 0 0'. Now I know the words of every one of the Beatles' hits and have practised often enough many a folk song on the piano, like 'Linden Lea' and 'Londonderry Air', but Glenn Miller? I've never heard this kind of band music, but I'm prepared to be open minded. Something tells me I'm going to get very familiar with it before the end of the week, as I notice Penny's pile of records contains two or three at most. Today I feel prepared for just about anything. I tell her about my Dansette record player at home and promise to have it brought down.

We decide to resume our unpacking. My room smells institutionally clean and there's that warmth again I noticed on my interview day. It wraps around you like a comforting blanket, unlike the coal fire at home, which burns on one side and sends chilly draughts on the other. I've never felt as warm as this in my whole life.

There's a break in Penny's music, probably while she turns over the record, and now I can tell there are people all around me, not far away. Coming from the floor above, I can hear a babble of girls' voices and an occasional shriek of laughter. Is it only a few hours since I first arrived? I feel as if I've been here ages.

Earlier today I stood outside on the pavement with my family and belongings around me looking up at Dale House, Number One College Road, my new home for three terms. At the end of a terrace, it's a late Victorian red-brick building, three storeys high, double-fronted with two bay windows. We entered by the rather grand front door up a set of stone steps. My mother, sister Judith and brother-in-law Pete came to cheer me on and manhandle two suitcases and the heavy old trunk. "What have you got in here, an elephant or just the kitchen sink?" said the ever-patient Pete.

Inside, Dale House proved to be a maze. Once through the front door, we were confronted with a myriad stairs and passages. We passed a common room with a television (which Judith said, helpfully, I would never have the time to watch), a telephone (which prompted my mother to tell me to ring at least once a week) and a set of pigeonholes (which Pete reminded me to look in every day for letters). After two flights of stairs, we had to negotiate several steps down, then bizarrely several steps up, until we arrived in my corridor at the back of the house, hauling the luggage with us. How I will ever find my way back down to the common room I have no idea.

Our destination was a long corridor made up of four fairly large bedrooms, two on each side, created with wooden partitions for walls and painted white. I found out that my room looks out onto the side road leading to the College, ideal for watching everyone passing by. The best thing is a lovely tree, with leaves just on the turn from green to hints of orange and red. Pete told me it's a cherry. There'll be white or even pink blossom in the spring, he said.

Each room accommodates two students, the College's instant solution to being forced to make at least one friend. To share among eight of us are a single bathroom and a separate toilet; another way of either making friends or causing potential problems. We have no such luxury of even a sink in our rooms, a privilege granted to third years only. For now, I am a fresh-faced first year, the lowest of the low with a lot to learn.

My mother inspected the ample wardrobes while Judith fussed over the making of my bed. We read the printed instructions together about what to do with the two sheets. After this first week, only one clean sheet was issued and one used sheet had to be put out into the corridor to be collected for washing. I couldn't make sense of it all, but Judith said, just to remember, top to bottom and bottom sheet out of the door. I supposed I would get the hang of it eventually. Then we spread Aunty Alice's red tartan rug over the blankets and immediately my room looked more homely.

As it was considered better for me to do my own packing and arrangement of my collection of posters on the blank pin board, the time came to bid farewell.

My mother said, for the umpteenth time, how she thought I would manage quite well. She would write lots of letters and I could phone her once a week. I made a mental note that I must find my way back to those pigeonholes and the telephone we'd passed earlier.

Sentiment does not rule our family. We don't cry or say how much we love each other. It's a 'chin up, shoulders back, get on with it' kind of love and I attribute my lack of homesickness to that. Despite being the last child to leave the nest, not once had my mother mentioned that she would miss me, or wonder what she would do without me, or who was going to run the messages on a Saturday, or lick out the bowl after she had put the cake mixture into the tin.

Selfishly, I had given no thought to the empty house which awaited her as I waved goodbye to the disappearing car. Perhaps that was as it should be.

And so, for me, tough love worked.

CHAPTER THREE

~~~

'WINDS THAT BLOW LONELY'

My first day of lectures. I discover that from now on, Education is spelt with a capital 'E' and I am going to spend three whole years learning about it. That's the most important and probably the only thing I'll remember by the end of today.

This morning begins with a round of meetings. The Principal and Vice Principal in turn give serious talks, the contents of which I forget immediately. It's all a bit of a haze really. First there are lists to check in the 'notices corridor'. Peering through a huddle of girls, all far taller than diminutive me, it's difficult enough to find my name for Main Subject tutorials and those so-important Education groups.

Scanning the list for 'Miss Amelia Hardy', I realise that when I'm a fully-fledged teacher, I shall be known as 'Miss Hardy'. It sounds rather grand. I feel excited already. And a bit hungry. That one overdone slice of toast at eight o'clock was definitely not enough. The smell of burning is still in my nose. I'm too excited and too hungry to concentrate.

Lunch in the middle of the day is a welcome distraction, as the hunger pangs well up even more. I stand for an age with a plastic tray in an endless queue, aromas of cabbage and strong brown gravy wafting towards me. My dinner consists of a nameless piece of meat, a heap of lumpy mashed potato and a few green beans which look far too soggy. I shall never turn my nose up again at my mother's vegetables, which I know are far tastier.

The next highlight is a compulsory look into the Porters' Lodge, a tiny office with a huge ledger. It is pointed out that this is where we must sign out before going into town in the evening and then sign in on return. Later than half ten, something called a late-night pass must be applied for and signed by the Principal, no less.

"Climbing in through windows or letting people in is not encouraged," warns the third year conducting the tour. I imagine by the mock severity of her voice that this has been tried on numerous occasions and is not about to stop any time soon. I'm not sure if I'd be brave enough to try it or have the inclination. Perhaps it's best if I stick to the rules.

And it's true that College is 'in loco parentis'. At home, my mother would stand on the front doorstep in the evening as the church clock struck ten, tapping her foot to the chimes. If my sister and her boyfriend appeared round the corner at the bottom of the street one minute later, there'd be war on. My own experience in that department is precisely nil.

This afternoon's timetable states that there are two more lectures: one in the Main Hall on Science (a subject I'm not keen on) and Art (which I am looking forward to). The Art one is to be held in the 'Lecture Block'. As I flounder along corridors among crowds of students, a helpful second year tells me it's not in the main building but is a few minutes' walk away, 'across the Lecture Block path'. Naturally. Wherever that is. I follow the direction of travel of the majority and eventually find it. It is on the very edge of the campus and built solidly of smooth red brick; I'm told it was formerly a grammar school. I instantly feel at home in the familiar style of its classrooms.

Then, at half past three, there is 'afternoon tea'. I can't quite believe it. I thought that was something the Queen had. But sure enough, I turn up at the dining hall and enjoy a jam sandwich on soft sliced white bread and a square of cake covered in pink icing, liberally sprinkled with coconut. I discover that this is indeed a daily occurrence. Something to look forward to at least, if lunch is a disaster.

With a great sense of relief, I make it to the end of the day's timetable and find my way back 'home' to Dale House. We don't use the front entrance as I did on my very first day here. Our entry is along the side road, into the cellar door, through the basement and up two flights of stairs leading to our corridor and my room.

I've collected a sheaf of papers on my lecture travels and I fling them on my desk with abandon. They land in a scattered heap. Then I collapse onto the bed, greeting my red tartan rug like an old friend. I have never been as tired as this. Well, perhaps the day of my last 'A' level exam comes a close second.

It feels as if the seven new faces I encountered just the other day are fast becoming my newly adopted family. My room-mate, who was the last to arrive, is, like Penny, from somewhere in Yorkshire. She seems friendly enough, but already says she can't wait for next weekend to get home to see her boyfriend. She's only here for the lectures and that's it, according to her conversation as we lay in our two single beds last night, talking in the dark. What a shame, I thought, although I didn't voice my opinion. She's going to miss out on the sheer fun of being away from home.

There've been tears from some of the girls as they sat around moping all yesterday afternoon, like children missing their mothers, which is something I cannot comprehend. I tried to console them: "Your mother hasn't gone anywhere. She'll still be there when you go home."

I told them a story from my childhood, how, when I was five, it was planned for me to stay at Aunty Alice's house overnight. (She's the one who gave me the tartan rug.) I cried so much that despite promises of a bacon sandwich for breakfast, my aunty had to take me home on the last bus. The reason I cried? My mother had simply disappeared out of the door after leaving me, without giving me her usual one kiss on the cheek. I was too young to explain that if only she'd said a 'proper' goodbye, I would have been quite happy. After that, I stayed lots of times and didn't mind at all being away from home, with many happy weekends and holidays at my paternal grandparents'.

There is love everywhere in our family: undeclared, but open-armed, northern and generous. It fills and satisfies me and I take it wherever I go. I have no need to weep for home. This weekend, my mother has given me a proper goodbye, that is, my one kiss on the cheek and a cheery wave. Why don't the others feel the same? It is a mystery to me.

So last night, to cheer everyone up, the third years who live on the floor above invited us all on our corridor to a folk club down in the town. I've only ever heard of such things, never been to one. Unlike most eighteen-year olds, a weekend outing for me has been the comparative safety of a sixth form dance in the school hall. However, in the interests of not only training to be a teacher but learning about life, I reckoned that I might as well start with the folk night. After all, there was safety in numbers, so I decided to become one of the 'crowd'.

The eight of us are a motley group. In particular, two big personalities make their presence felt. Penny, my next-door neighbour, the Glenn Miller fan, strides along in masculine fashion and wears a short dark red dressing gown, complete with silk sash, rather in the style of a smoking jacket. I haven't the courage to ask her why she doesn't just wear a coat like other people, but I gather she likes to rummage round jumble sales.

Mary, her room-mate, with a round face and short, curly, ginger hair, laughs and jokes all the time. She comes from my corner of the world and I think North-Easterners do tend to have a laid-back, carefree sort of attitude. I'm not sure if I actually fit into that category. More of a worrier, myself. Mary does not appear to be one of those.

Both girls have a straight way of speaking, of saying exactly what they think. It would be so easy for me to be in awe of them with their outgoing, confident ways, but I detect that underneath lies hidden a wealth of genuine concern and friendliness. And we do share a common goal: we all want to become teachers.

Nevertheless, I still wonder how I am ever going to fit into this crowd.

After dutifully 'signing out' at the Porters' Lodge, we found the folk club a smoky, beery affair. Some of the group chose to order cider, but when it came to my turn,

I elected to drink lemonade, to be on the safe side. I have never had the money, inclination or even the opportunity to try anything alcoholic. Unless you count an extremely small glass of sherry at Christmas during a family game of Monopoly. The bubbles of my lemonade spat and popped into my face, and most disconcertingly, up my nose. But I kept on sipping and smiling, determined to look as if I was enjoying the whole thing.

We sat on high stools in the bar and listened to verse after verse of songs apparently written around only three chords. Most of the audience seemed to know every word, joining in with gusto in the choruses. The only one I can remember begins 'Four strong winds that blow lonely'. The tune is still whirling round in my head today. It's a bit mournful. I'm not sure if the evening really did much to cheer up the homesick girls.

Amid the noise and the smoke, I looked in turn at each new face of my fellow students and wondered if I'd find anything in common with any one of them. What about outgoing Penny, or Mary who comes out with the most hilarious things? Less than two days ago, they were all strangers. And today, I still have to find out about Jill at the end of the corridor, who has two long, dark plaits, and how Fran, in the room opposite mine, came to have the exotic-sounding Italian name of Francesca Bosco.

It's the end of the first week and many of my earlier fears have been laid to rest. The eight of us have discovered that it is much easier to find out about each other if we all congregate in one room. For some reason, it's usually Penny's, which she shares with Mary. There are only two chairs, but we make full use of the beds and the floor. We talk about everything and anything each night until the small hours: our homes, our families and the medicals we had to pass to get here.

Penny was asked by her doctor to bring in a urine sample in a bottle. Having no idea of the amount required, she decided to play it safe and took a pop bottle full to the top, carrying it to the doctor's surgery on the bus. We laughed until our sides ached and the tears ran down our cheeks.

Jill still holds dear two old, cloth rabbits given to her as a baby. She can't be parted from them and so they live on her bed in her room, propped up on the pillows.

Fran, who has long, free-flowing brown hair, has Italian grandparents and hails from the south of England. She is continually scoffed at for her accent, but insists she isn't a Cockney, as she was born many miles away from London, but to no avail. To our northern ears, either Durham or Yorkshire, anyone who says 'now' instead of 'no' or 'Oi'm gowing to 'ave a barf', definitely must be a Cockney. Mary remarks, pronouncing the 'a' of 'bath' as in apple, "I could have had a bath by the time you've said 'barf'".

Seven of us agree that, in our opinion, Fran hasn't been fully educated. There is outrage when she asks what a dry-stone wall is. She says she's never heard of them before and we are quick to tell her that they criss-cross the fells and hills of the north and she should get out more. According to Fran, she has spent every holiday of her life in Italy. Our little town of Bishopsfield, where we all now live, is the furthest north she has ever ventured. Thus a great deal of friendly scorn is heaped upon her by us northern girls.

It is fortunate that we have not been similarly quizzed on our knowledge of the far distant south, as we would most certainly be found wanting.

CHAPTER FOUR

~~~

DISTRACTIONS

Chin in hand, I doodle with a pencil on a blank sheet of file paper. As the table in my room has to act as both a study desk and a dining table, it is littered with a bewildering array of objects, which do little to aid my concentration.

Legitimate items include scissors, glue, a roll of sticky-back plastic, a battered but much-loved pencil case I have used since the Lower Sixth, an even older wooden ruler and a pile of unopened education books, newly acquired from Bryden's, the bookshop.

Distracting me is the aroma from an opened packet of white sliced bread and the sight of an unopened packet of digestives, just waiting to be broken into. Then, lying among the debris and pricking my conscience, is yesterday's letter from Mam in a fat cream envelope, as yet unread.

The table sits at right angles to the window, which acts as another distraction. While I attempt to concentrate, I end up gazing out past the cherry tree and across the road to a handsome late Victorian detached house, the residence of our esteemed principal, Miss Pringle.

At our very first introductory lecture, I was mesmerised by her silver-grey hair, neatly tied up in a smooth bun, not a strand out of place. Her prim, almost severe demeanour, which I first encountered in the portrait on the wall in main College on that interview day, rendered me in awe of her and I have discovered that even the die-hard third years feel the same. After that initial appearance, she is only to be seen in the confines of her private wood-panelled office on rare occasions, we're told. At the end of every year, each one of us will be required to knock on her door, enter that hallowed room and discover what progress we're making as fledgling teachers. I can feel the trepidation already.

And if I don't make a start with this essay soon, my career will be over before it has even begun.

Opposite me is the biggest distraction of all. While our respective room-mates would rather enjoy the company of boyfriends at home every weekend, I had the idea of Fran and I working together for company. However, trying to write at each end of the table in the same room is not proving very successful, both space-wise and the fact that conversation never ceases.

I sweep the bread and biscuit packets to one side to

spread out my papers. The essay I am tussling with has the title, 'What do you expect to gain from your college experience?'

Thoughtfully, I reach for my old ruler and underline it. Then I decide to write some rough notes, so I write 'Outline' and underline that.

"Does your education group have to do this?" I ask Fran.

She grins. "No fear! I wouldn't dare answer that. Does it mean educationally or personally? I mean, do you expect to gain a teaching certificate or a boyfriend?"

"Be serious. Miss Brooks gave us this title. I doubt she has had a boyfriend in her life. In fact, she is the most timid, uninspiring lecturer or teacher I have ever encountered."

Fran nods. "Most likely she's been harassed to death in school by unruly, undisciplined children and fled here to the safety of St Mag's."

I continue my complaining, mainly because I can't think of the opening sentence, let alone the first paragraph. "How on earth do I know what I'll gain when I have no idea what the courses are going to be about? I haven't met half the lecturers yet or been into school. What a ridiculous question!"

Fran holds up her notebook. "I've got to write about what took place during the first hundred thousand years in the history of mankind. Well, I mean, who was around to see?" She sharpens her pencil furiously. I watch the shavings flutter across the table. Fran has even less instinct for tidiness than I have.

"Wish I'd never chosen History for main." Her eyes swivel dreamily towards the window and the cherry tree. "I could have done Art." Seconds later, she resumes the sharpening until the lead breaks. "But then I can't stand pottery. Actually, I hate painting as well. At least I wouldn't have had to write long, boring essays though."

"Maybe not," I point out, jabbing my pencil in the air for effect. "But you'd have been up all night making models of Grisedale Abbey."

"Why's that?"

"They're mad on it," I reply, with the air of one who knows. "Every theme in every subject revolves around Grisedale Abbey. One of the third years told me. If you're not drawing it, you're following the course of the river that runs alongside or reliving the life of a monk."

Fran makes a face.

"It's either that or the village of Moreton," I go on, keen to let her know that my work is also piling up. "That's where our Environmental Studies is going to be based, I heard yesterday. The college bus is going to be back and forth every Monday. Anyway, you think History's bad: I've got to read a Graham Greene novel for next week for main English. That's going to be torture enough."

And we sit here, contentedly wallowing in our grumblings, without having written one word.

There follows a period of silence, during which I finally concoct my opening sentence. The first essay is going to take longer than I expected.

"This has to be in on Monday," I agonise. "I don't want to have to spend the whole weekend over it."

Fran looks up. "You're the lucky one. Mine should have been in this morning."

We grin at each other and try to concentrate on our respective tasks. This doesn't last long.

"Hi there, you two very studious people." Jill breezes in and stands at the open doorway, looking triumphant. As a main History girl like Fran, she has obviously already handed in her essay. "I've just been over to the library and happened to pass the notices corridor. And guess what? A list of names has just gone up for Teaching Practice."

We throw down our pencils to give her our full attention.

"Amelia, you're in Moreton Village School, starting next week."

My face falls. "Gosh, I didn't think we'd be thrown in at the deep end this early."

"Don't worry. Penny's name is beside yours. You're there together."

Now she comes nearer and leans on the table. "Hope you fancy fish and chips. We've just sent Mary down for six lots."

Our scattered papers catch her eye. She picks up

Fran's scribbled notes. "What *are* you doing? You've missed three noughts off the title of your essay. It's the first hundred *million* years you're supposed to write about!"

I make a tactful exit to switch on the kettle, Jill shakes her head in reproach and Fran snaps her pencil in half.

CHAPTER FIVE

~~~

'SAIL ON SILVER GIRL'

We glide smoothly and quietly across the hall floor to the warm, mellow tones of Vaughan Williams' 'Greensleeves'. Clad in regulation black leotards and tights, we twist and turn to the music, caressing the air with delicate hands. I curl low down, I reach up high, chin in the air. I can feel the hardness of the floor with my bare feet and my head is filled with the melody. I love every minute of it.

My introduction to Creative Movement or 'Dance' as it is called here in the Education world, has been quite revealing. Firstly, the official attire enhances some figures more than others. I can safely say that most of us have never moved creatively in our lives before. Furthermore, from what I have seen up to now, there are a few who don't intend to. Then I have found that it requires putting aside inhibitions, reacting towards other people and 'feeling' the music with your whole body. This requires not only physical work but courage.

Although it's a totally new subject for me, I take to it like a duck to water. Lacking in height as I am, any sort of PE in school found me lurking in the furthest corners of both the gym and the playing field. In netball, no one would throw the ball to me, as I couldn't possibly make a goal. In hockey, I confined myself to jogging up and down the sidelines, a safe distance away from flying sticks. A rap on the shins is no joy in the hockey season, with our exposed knees turning red raw in the midst of winter. Then in the gym, I could neither climb more than two feet up the ropes nor vault over the horse. And the buck defeated me completely.

But Dance is proving a different story.

As new students, we sit cross-legged on the floor like a class of seven-year olds and are told to, 'Listen to the music and think how you could move to it'.

This is my kind of language: no fear of physical injury, no impossible feats to surmount. After we finish our gliding, caressing and curling, we reach the climax of the lesson, making communal shapes and patterns. Then comes the final part, called 'limbering down'. We have to gracefully 'fold in our petals and sink into the ground'. I am totally engrossed.

Maths tells a similar tale. There is no wrestling with algebraic equations or terrible tangents and cosines. Who on earth needs them anyway? Instead we make block graphs using sticky coloured paper; we sort beads and shells to make sets. Next week, it's tessellations. Do circles fit together? No. Do squares fit together? Yes. So, we begin to understand how five-year olds learn mathematics.

And the day allocated to our main subjects is like a jug of water in the desert. I hang on to every word the lecturers give us in my main English: about themes and characters, heroes and anti-heroes, descriptive words and purple passages. There are treats in store: war poetry, Victorian poetry, Jane Austen's novels, all six of them. And tutorials on Thomas Hardy. What bliss this is for me: discovering new worlds in old subjects.

Along with the others, I revel in the swapping of comments about lecturers when we all gather in one of our rooms at the end of the day. I complain as eagerly as the rest about the amount of work to be done and that essay which is due in the day after tomorrow and not even the title written yet.

When lectures are done, we march down into town on the pretence of ordering the latest education book from Bryden's. It isn't really a pretence: we do have to buy lists of books for each subject. It gives us the excuse to spend a good hour rummaging around the dusty shelves on the third floor where the second-hand books are displayed.

Bryden's isn't a glossy sort of bookshop, where bestsellers hit you in the eye as you open the door, where, on asking for Homer's *Odyssey*, a weedy-looking assistant who knows nothing of the classics, gives you a blank stare as if you have dropped from another planet.

On the contrary, Bryden's has a bow window frontage and a door with a bell which jangles as you enter the engaging, fascinating shop. Every classic and great name in literature can be found here, children's books for all ages, picture books for the Nursery: all of which keeps us involved for many a long hour. Then, after browsing on all three floors, we finally decide on a five-shilling paperback of stories and rhymes for the under sevens, ready for Teaching Practice.

At each visit, I resolve that if I don't make it as a teacher, I will open just such a bookshop of my own.

Tearing ourselves away, we emerge cross-eyed and dizzy to wend our way up to the market to look for bargains in jumpers among the busy stalls. On the way, we have time to scrabble through a great pile of postcards in the art shop and on a stand outside the next-door establishment selling antiques and miscellaneous junk, we discover a cut-price record for a shilling.

Not being over endowed with cash, we have found an uncanny ability to purchase quirky gifts for the merest amount. Yesterday I came across a miniature chest of drawers made out of matchboxes, each drawer with a tiny ring for a handle. The outside is decorated so prettily with scenes of Bishopsfield that I shall put it aside as a perfect Christmas present for my grandmother.

Afterwards we enjoy a pot of milky coffee in the Elizabethan café, soaking in the atmosphere of the aged black timbers and exposed wattle and daub.

Our weekly provisions are few: digestive biscuits, instant coffee, tea bags and a tin of powdered milk, to offset any hunger pangs after Friday's dodgy meal in the dining hall of rubbery beefburgers and hard chips.

Sometimes we scoot straight down into town then, to another favourite café above a cake shop. We really liven up that little place, chattering and laughing up the narrow twisty stairs. Spreading out our shopping and books over the largest table, or two pushed together, depending on the number of our group, we demolish plates piled high with chips, cooked just as our mothers would make them. The added bonus is that they are the cheapest item on the menu.

We pity the regular customers, who must sigh with relief when we finally vacate that otherwise quiet spot. But, in our defence, we inhabit a world where we are carefree of any responsibility, other than for ourselves and our studies. Little do we know of husbands or houses or babies. We ignore the grey-haired pensioners and the harassed mothers tut-tutting over their china cups of tea about rowdy students.

Some people say that no one is aware of the moments when they are happy. I must be the exception to the rule, for I am certain that I do know. Each of these passing days is special. I will remember them as keenly and as clearly as all the words on Fran's Simon and Garfunkel LP 'Bridge Over Troubled Water', it's never been off the turntable. I am that 'silver girl' sailing on. The only troubled waters I see ahead are the hurdles to leap over, with the nagging feeling that I might trip over one of them, as a young student teacher.

Perhaps the highest of all might be the perennial question, trivial as it is – would anyone ask me to dance in the hall next Saturday night?

CHAPTER SIX

~~~~~

HUNGER PANGS

A few weeks into the first term and today, a most extraordinary thing has happened, and it has happened to me, wouldn't say boo to a goose, unassuming little Amelia. I must explain this use of the word 'extraordinary'. For any other eighteen-year old it would be the most ordinary, expected event.

It began this morning, with a discussion about the weekly Saturday night dance in the main hall: something no self-respecting student would miss, apart from those with at-home boyfriends. Fran and I never see our room-mates from after the final lecture on a Friday until late Sunday evening. Penny and Mary usually announce a 'date' they have lined up, which then leaves four of us to form a small posse to invade the dance floor together. As I mentioned earlier, there's safety in numbers.

We have been informed, courtesy of the wisdom of the upstairs third years, that a new influx of students always brings in a crowd of male spectators. St Margaret's, being a female College, attracts several young men from a nearby RAF base - our first intake this year of twenty-five male students hardly counts among a few hundred women. These officers, or aspiring pilots-to-be, line the edges of the dance hall every Saturday night, assessing the dozens of females who are unattached. They remind me of little boys eyeing up the display in a sweet shop window before stepping inside to claim their favourite.

Our little posse of four is made up of Jill, her room-mate Pat, Fran and me. Dressed in nothing too outrageous, simply jeans and a cream blouse, I am hoping to disappear among the myriad bodies, constantly moving to the beat of the music.

A band is up on the stage, belting out at full volume a cover version of 'American Pie'. With miming gestures, we point to a vacant spot on the dance floor, deposit our handbags and proceed to do a kind of shuffling war dance around them. I've discovered that this is one of Jill's favourite songs and so we move with extra gusto, completely absorbed in joining in the words: 'Bye, bye, Miss American Pie'. I have no idea what the words mean, but I toss my long fair hair to the music while Jill shakes her dark mane.

Out of the corner of my eye, I see a group of four men stride purposefully across from the edge of the hall, obviously RAF by their gait and smart appearance: not your average long-haired students in flared jeans with patches. They ask us if we would like to dance with them.

Perhaps because of my stature, I have attracted a young man who is similarly short, at least in RAF terms. He is of unremarkable appearance: hair light brown, closely cut, wears a tidy suit and I notice a countenance not displeasing, but with no hint of a smile.

My heart soars. This is part of my college education, as I have fully expected and the order of things, is it not? There has been little opportunity so far in my life. End of term gatherings at school were all perfectly innocent. Girls over here, boys over there. Mostly, never the twain shall meet.

Now, I have been brought up in an all-female household. For me, men and boys are totally unknown territory. Father, grandfather and favourite uncle have all been taken away from me; the first unreasonably died too young; the second reached an allotted life span of little more than three score years and ten, leaving me with only a few early memories; the third was whisked away by a wife, far more attractive than a needy seven-year-old niece.

For the moment, while the music plays, I am enjoying myself. We dance together for the rest of the evening. No turning away after the first or second dance with a polite "thank you and goodbye". He even takes me to the anteroom just off the main hall where cups of coffee and glasses of coke can be had, to restore our dancing energy. There's no alcohol on the premises, as most of us are under the age of twenty-one, although before the next election, the age of majority is to be reduced to eighteen and so then alcohol need not be off-limits. I don't know when College will catch up though.

My ears feel dulled after the thudding of the drums, but at least we can hear ourselves speak. I find out that his name is Keith and he comes from somewhere in Lancashire. I smile politely and try to breathe more normally. It feels as if we have been dancing for hours and my feet are starting to ache.

Back to the hall we go to resume our place on the floor. Everyone dances wildly to 'Good Vibrations', although the band are a poor second best to the Beach Boys, and then we all join in at the tops of our voices with 'The House of the Rising Sun'.

I know what comes next: a mass exodus across to all the Halls of Residence. Each man who escorts a partner back is deemed to be 'lucky'. Or is it perhaps the women who are lucky enough to have held on to their dance partners until the music stopped? Either way, my feelings are a jumble.

Who is this bloke anyway? Beyond the simple facts of his name and where he comes from, I know nothing about him, nor does he know me. We are little more than strangers who happen to have been dancing opposite each other all evening.

The visiting group plays its last reverberating chord and the drummer crashes and thumps his drums until we all turn to clap and cheer. A few of the men let out piercing whistles. I'm relieved for more than one reason. My feet have had enough.

I retrieve my handbag and look round. Jill, Pat and Fran must have long ago retreated to the safety of their rooms in Dale House, as there's no sign of them now. And goodness knows where Penny and Mary are. They were 'lucky' to start with, as they already had 'dates'. If it was school, I would say, they are behind the bike sheds. Metaphorically speaking.

I have no option but to take Keith's proffered hand and allow him to lead me outside into the dark night. We walk together silently along the paths between the neatly cut lawns and past the White Gates, a white-painted five-barred gate which leads onto the side road next to Dale House. A couple is leaning against one of the posts, oblivious to the world, arms round each other. They must be passionately in love, I think, or it certainly looks like it.

But something feels wrong.

How can you tell from a blurred face in the dark and ten minutes over a cup of coffee whether you like someone or not?

I glance up at him. He keeps looking straight ahead. He doesn't smile or wink at me. We reach our destination: that rather grand Victorian front door of Dale House. I mutter hastily, thank you and goodbye. Does he expect me to kiss someone I only met a few hours ago? I have only ever given my own mother a perfunctory kiss at bedtime or when leaving the house. I can't remember ever kissing my sister and in my no-nonsense upbringing, it is unknown to hug anyone, either relations or friends, let alone a stranger. Emotions have to be held in. That's the unsaid, underlying rule in my North-East coal mining town. Tears have to be dried up quickly, or as one of my older aunts would say, 'I'll give you something to cry about'. She was born way back in Edwardian times, but these mantras are still passed on. No amount of so-called 1960s 'free love' that you see on films and on television these days, has yet to break into them, at least not in my family circles.

I have yet to witness any tears from my mother, who lost her husband after only eight years of marriage and was left to bring up a seven-year old and a newly born baby alone. Life is hard and you must learn to take it and carry on. Children are not pampered. Loved, yes, but in a disciplined way. The words 'I love you' have never passed my lips in speaking to any member of the family and have never been said to me. But I know that everyone does love me. I just know.

And so I have no reason to kiss or show any affection for this man who has walked me 'home'. This is no love across the dance floor moment. Perhaps he thinks it is. For him, maybe. For me, absolutely not.

Poor deluded Keith. He must think I'm playing hard to catch.

To my surprise, as I turn the brass handle of the front door, he quickly asks me if he can see me again the next day.

I can't form the word 'no'. After all, I suppose, it would be exciting to be called upon and to be able to tell the others all about it. At the last second I agree, before I dive through the doorway, into the maze of corridors and up and down the various flights of stairs to reach the back of the house and our haven of four rooms.

Because we are so much out on a limb, away from the rest of the house in our own corridor, we gel together like a little family. We all know at any one time where each other is and what each one is doing.

Jill, Pat and Fran, who indeed returned earlier, are bursting to find out everything. All three of them are in my room, waiting.

"Well, what's his name?"

"Fancy you, dancing with one man, all night!"

"When are you seeing him again? Come on, Amelia, out with it!"

I smile sheepishly and feel my old teenage habit returning, of blushing a glowing shade of pink. But I tell them as much as I know. Comments of admiration are heaped upon me. The partners of the other girls had all gone their separate ways after just the first dance.

The heated, noisy excitement of all the gossip brings

down the third years from upstairs. They sound equally impressed.

"I can't believe quiet you, having a boyfriend already!"

I protest that he isn't quite 'a boyfriend', but no one is listening. Only Penny is more cynical. "Just be careful, my little Amelia," she warns.

She has been out with, it seems to me, umpteen men: a different one every Saturday so far, not counting the wild life she has apparently lived throughout the sixth form. I think Leeds must be an altogether different place from my home town. It's much bigger for a start.

"I know what I'm talking about," she admonishes gravely. "Don't you go throwing yourself at him."

Little does she know I have done no throwing myself of any sort and have no intention of doing so.

Tonight, as I write today's remarkable events into my diary, I surprise myself by feeling quite pleased by all the attention and remarks, now that I have made it to the rank of 'having a boyfriend'. Anyone who is male and calls for you on the phone or at the door is regarded as such, so I can hardly continue to deny it. Whoever he is, he has danced with me, has been suitably impressed or attracted and is coming back for more.

Three weeks have passed and I have suffered. During the day, I can hardly eat. Not love sickness, however vehemently my corridor mates argue it is. On the contrary,

I have decided I am suffering from a severe case of fright. It's true that I enjoy the general aura of 'going out', but when the moment comes and Jill or Fran pop their heads round the door with a cheerful grin and say, "He's here," then the torture begins.

The blushing spreads from my cheeks and neck and even down my arms. Meanwhile, I don't know what in the world to talk about. We don't laugh. I haven't skipped or hitched once: a habit I have never grown out of since childhood. Then come the stony, still silences on the late evening doorstep. This is not my idea of a romance.

Tonight, Keith announces that he is going home for the weekend and would I like to come and meet his Mum and his sisters? I realise I should take this as a compliment. I should welcome his invitation to get to know him properly, in a homely situation. Perhaps that is his reasoning.

As it is, fear of the unknown has taken hold of me. I make my apologies here and now, giving the excuse that my own mother is expecting me home, although actually she is not. I say that this is not working out between us, privately thinking that nothing had ever started. I prattle on, probably talking far more than I have ever done in his company.

Luckily for me, he agrees, whether thankfully or not, I can't tell.

After parting on the doorstep, I skip all the way back to my room. I feel destined never to meet Keith again.

Perhaps he will never be seen at any future College dances. It has been no Romeo and Juliet story. I want a friend, or at least someone who would begin by being a friend, who wouldn't mind what I say, even if it is the first silly thought which comes into my head, like, 'Is my petticoat showing at the back?' I am looking for someone who would like me for who I am, someone I feel comfortable with and most importantly, someone to have fun with.

Where would I find anyone like that?

Tonight, now that this escapade is all over, I am happy to sit on the bed and describe to Jill, Fran and company a picture of my ideal partner. They joke that this person does not exist. I maintain that one day their joke will backfire and I will find this elusive man.

Just before I write up the events in my diary, it is heartening for me to finish the evening, sitting on my red tartan rug, propped up with pillows, demolishing several slices of buttered toast. My hunger pangs have returned.

CHAPTER SEVEN

~~~

INTO THE FRAY

The time has come when we must be initiated into Teaching Practice and we're all dreading it - strange, because we've each chosen to train to be teachers, yet we are daunted by the huge task ahead.

And so, early on a dismally dark Monday morning, we are travelling to the various villages in the Dale, the minibus dropping off groups of us at each school for the first day of our first classroom encounter. Normally I would relish a scenic drive into the countryside, but this contraption with the official title of 'the College Minibus' has no hint of luxury or vestige of comfort about it at all. It is basically a black metal box on wheels with worn grey leather seats. After five minutes into the journey, they feel like blocks of wood. This so-called bus must have been in use since at least as far back as the nineteen fifties and

College hasn't seen any need to replace it, obviously being of the opinion that students don't deserve soft seats.

Our driver seems to be in the utmost hurry and flings his vehicle round each bend at an alarming speed. We hang on tightly to our rolled-up posters, lesson plan files and bags overflowing with display items. I grasp the nearest floor-to-roof chrome pole to prepare for the next 'golden bump'. And here it comes, as the bus tops yet another rise in the road. For a split second, the wheels hang in mid-air before landing on the tarmac. We count seven bumps, and seven times our stomachs lurch up to our hearts. Perhaps the reason for the feelings of queasiness is partly the anticipation of what is to come, of standing alone and fearful in a classroom in front of twenty-eight expectant upturned faces.

I hang on for dear life and stare out of the bus window, having crazy thoughts. If only I could just for this morning be transformed into a cow in a field. Happily chewing the cud, I would not have a care in the world. This venture of training to be a teacher must be driving me insane, I think. When will I be able to walk into a school, carefree and confident? I cannot envisage that day. Now that I am to be responsible for the education of all these children, even for just a few hours, I am desperately afraid.

Maybe I shouldn't have bothered with breakfast, such as it was. A digestive biscuit dunked into a cup of watery tea flavoured with powdered milk had to suffice this morning. Hauling myself out of bed to rush over to the dining hall in time for proper scrambled eggs was asking too much. As it was, I just made it to the wretched bus with only a minute to spare.

As I watch the green fields flying by in a blur, I have completely forgotten any of the reasons I initially had for choosing this career path. To make matters worse, I will have two friends in the same classroom looking on, waiting their turns. Yes, for some strange reason, the powers-that-be have deemed our first Teaching Practice should be shared. Perhaps they think they are letting us in gently. It seems a ridiculous surplus of student teachers, especially as there are fewer than thirty pupils in our charge. I have been teamed up with Penny from my corridor, and Alison, a new friend, who is in my main English group.

Our destination on this Monday morning journey and our first stop is Moreton, a small country town nestled at the foot of the Dales. Our black box on four wheels creaks and groans to a halt and the three of us clamber out, weighed down with bags stuffed with teaching aids. Our impatient driver reminds us to be here at this exact spot at four o'clock on the dot for the return journey. With a crunch of gears, the tin bus disappears round the corner, carrying the rest of the students on their way further up the Dale.

We grasp our belongings and turn our faces towards the fray.

Moreton School is a Victorian stone building, huddled in the corner of a large, windy marketplace. The old school bell still hangs in its niche above the front door, with leaded windows on either side. All the houses in the square are built of stone, some of them small cottages, others with three storeys, built for the gentry. In one corner stands the church with its enormous spire. Opposite us, I can see a sweet shop, a chemist's and a café offering a cup of tea and a scone for one shilling and sixpence. But none of these delights is meant for us today and we head towards the side entrance of the school which we've been told to use.

In the playground at the back, overlooking rolling green fields, three classes of noisy children aged from five to eleven years old skip, jump and run about. I have never heard such a great, overwhelming noise. Two or three of the smallest girls and boys stand motionless around the edge of the yard, holding their mothers' hands, looking on. They look just the way I feel: reluctant to join in the mass of whirling, moving bodies, happy simply to observe and weigh up the situation before launching into the frenzy.

There is no time to indulge in any of these emotions, as there's a lot to do before nine o'clock. We are to take Art with the class of mixed infants, that is, boys and girls aged five, six and seven. I imagine the children will think this is a great relief from the usual round of writing and mental arithmetic.

In the classroom, after the chill of the unheated college bus, we huddle around the huge wire guard which protects the rows of old wooden desks from the flames of the open coal fire. There's an odd combination of smells. As the three of us warm our hands, taking in our surroundings, I guess it must be soot from the chimney mingled with the disinfectant from the regularly cleaned floor. Generations have been taught here for over a hundred years: they learnt to read from large print readers, perhaps some of them from the very same dog-eared copies adorning the bookstand here, judging by their decades-old illustrations. They sharpened their pencils into the same waste-paper basket and no doubt spilt their paint onto these actual wooden floorboards.

High up on the wall, the clock with its big clear numbers looks down on us, its pointers clicking inevitably towards the hour. There are innumerable jobs to be done and no time to marvel at the fact that we are but a tiny fraction of the history of this country school.

As we work feverishly to be ready on the hour, Miss Dodds, the class teacher, makes an appearance and sits at her high, old-fashioned teacher's desk watching us, looking bemused. She keeps peering up across a diminishing pile of brown arithmetic books, red pen in hand, expertly ticking and crossing.

We put out paints and brushes, glue and scissors, even little saucers of real sand and shells. Our topic is 'The Sea'. On my first weekend trip home to the north-east coast I spent hours on the beach, collecting bucketfuls of pebbles, seaweed and driftwood, plus two shells of dead crabs. My prize possession, courtesy of an uncle who has a friend with a fishing boat down the docks, was the empty, rounded shell of a sea urchin. I thought its raised dots were a fine example of pattern and texture, the subject of our latest Art lecture. The shell was so inspiring that I forgave its faint, whiffy smell of salty fish.

Back at College, the three of us painstakingly wrote labels, painted a picture of a lighthouse and begged and borrowed postcards of the seaside. Now we pin and position with care all our items, matched with the correct labels. And to complete the display, we arrange a length of blue crepe paper to represent the sea.

We stand back and survey our handiwork, then look at each other with smug smiles on our faces. I reckon the art the children produce today is going to be easily the best when we discuss it at our next Education lecture.

The sound of the school bell clanging outside on the windswept yard interrupts our thoughts. In come our pupils for the morning, bringing in the fresh, clean air with them, faces shining, hair dishevelled. In contrast to the wild disorder we witnessed on the playground, not a word is spoken here in the classroom. Eyes are wide open, looking up and down at the three interlopers who have intruded upon their territory.

After a command from Miss Dodds, I marvel at how obediently they each sit at their places, arms folded, not touching any of the art materials in front of them. But I can tell from the expression on their faces that each one is excited at the prospect of what is to come.

The calling of the register and the collection of the children's dinner money seem to take up a large proportion of time, and at last, Miss Dodds gives us a nod as the sign that we can begin.

Penny, famous for her dressing gown cum coat, is today in school teacher mode, wearing a more sober skirt and jumper. She was elected earlier by Alison and me to introduce the topic. We reckoned her usual confident manner would get us off to a good start. But it is a nerve-racking moment even for her.

"This is a display about the sea," she begins hesitantly. "Who has been to the seaside?"

Fewer than half of the hands shoot up. The rest of the children, probably from remote farms and cottages up in the hills, look blank. Too late, I realise that it would take hours to get to Scarborough from here.

"What shall I say next?" she mouths to me. I push a shell into her hand.

"Show them this," I mutter. Tentatively, she holds up the shell.

"You might find something like this if you are walking along the beach. Or pebbles, crabs..."

Fumbling for each object in turn, she forgets she has her back to her young audience. Necks crane, knees are up on chairs, until finally in desperation, Penny announces, "Now, you may come and look at the display."

As one body, the entire class of twenty-eight children rises and hurtles to the front, pushing Alison and me aside and knocking Penny flat across the display table. Pebbles, shells, dead crabs and the precious sea urchin are fingered, tossed and finally scattered. Labels are mixed up and the blue crepe paper we had so carefully arranged to depict the sea is creased and torn at the edges.

"Right everyone! Back to your seats!"

Miss Dodds is standing up behind her desk and thunders out the command.

As the last little body departs we emerge, crumpled, harassed and totally trodden under. No one has ever told us, and it certainly has never entered our inexperienced heads, to invite only one group at a time to look and examine in an orderly manner. They say one learns by one's mistakes and if we have learned anything today, then this is surely one big lesson in organisation.

Somehow, we set the class off on their artistic pursuits. Soon, brushes are flying, paint pots totter and sheets of paper are covered in what I am sure are unbelievable works of art. It takes all three of us to get round the working groups to write Christian names in our best, newly-perfected printing style on every piece of paper. To each child, we say, "Tell me about your picture."

That done, I glance at the clock and realise it is high time we were clearing up. Goodness knows how long that will take, with only five minutes of the lesson remaining before playtime.

Now it is my turn to show my inbred teacher's style. I position myself in the middle of the rows of desks, survey the busy children and open my mouth to tell them all to stop working. But to my utter and eternal shame, no sound or squeak comes forth. My voice has gone out of production, gone on strike, folded up on me. How am I going to speak to all twenty-eight at once? None of them are looking at me. All are still painting, cutting and glueing, and making quite a din while they are doing it. How can I get this ever-turning human machinery to become silent and motionless? This is a task beyond me.

My salvation comes from on high.

"Right! Stop everyone!"

Once again, the booming order is issued from the elevated teacher's desk next to the warm fire. Then the voice continues quietly and calmly, "Put down your paintbrush, your scissors, whatever you have in your hand and look at me."

Like a magic trick, the hubbub ceases, as the children, every single one of them, lay down their implements and all eyes swivel towards the owner of the commanding voice, their class teacher.

I wish a huge, gaping hole in the classroom would swallow me into oblivion.

Another huge lesson learnt.

CHAPTER EIGHT

~~~

TWO DIFFERENT WORLDS

Now the days are foggy and damp and a mellow, colourful autumn is slowly showing signs of the beginnings of winter. But the wind is not so keen and the air is a gentle, cold presence, unlike the biting, whipping lash of the North Sea winds that I am used to.

Yesterday, for Art, we collected sycamore, oak and horse-chestnut leaves, yellow, red and orangey brown, and pressed them under piles of thick education books. In English, we tried our hand at writing poems about the dying of the summer, which I have always thought to be such a sad, regretful subject.

Fran, who is from the depths of the south, complains about this chilly northern region. To compensate, she continually wears at least two jumpers. Mary and I exaggerate mercilessly about how freezing the North-East is. We laugh and say she has been brought up a 'southern softie'. Here in Bishopsfield, in the winter, the snow does not lie long or deep, or so I've been told. The town lies in a hollow, which explains why it is not seen from a distance. Instead, you approach it unawares. Over the brow of a hill, the road drops down and the houses and the winding river open up before you.

A few miles up into the Dales, it's a different story. The winters are much harsher there, so one of the upstairs third years said; she spent five gruelling weeks on Teaching Practice last year, travelling in snow and ice. We are sheltered at St Mag's on the edge of a plain.

I think about my recent forage along the beach at home for our infamous classroom display, picking up pebbles with freezing cold fingers. Even in October, the sea can be grey and angry. The winds from Scandinavia whip up the waves and colour my cheeks and nose red. Much as I love breathing in lungfuls of whole oxygen with the taste of salt on my lips, I have instead found a new passion for the mild and gentle air of the green countryside.

As if to test my loyalty, for the last week, a fog has enveloped us. It seems as if it is wrapped around the College buildings like a muffler, trapping and preventing us from escape. But eventually we do escape, back to our old familiar homes for a half term's holiday: a whole week to spend in the comforting bosom of our families. From one world to another, it seems.

In the kitchen, drying the Sunday breakfast dishes while my mother, hands clad in yellow rubber gloves in her usual place, washes up at the sink, I slip back with ease into younger daughter role. There is a joint of brisket cooking slowly in the oven and the old radio is churning out 'Family Favourites' in the background. Judith and Pete will be here for dinner soon and the Yorkshire puddings are still to mix.

It would have been so easy to have been the one who stayed at home with our widowed mother, fulfilling duties as kitchen maid, shopper, duster of the ornaments and polisher of the piano keys. But I have two weapons in my armoury. The first one is Judith, my 'big' sister, big only in the sense that she was born before me. In height there is not much between us, probably an inch or two, me being the taller, if you can call under five feet 'tall'. She paved the way, by leaving home seven years ago to start her teacher training.

The second weapon I am blessed with is the fact that my mother has always been good at pushing us along – forward, onward, onto the next step of life, 'En Avant' as our grammar school motto urged, the school all three of us attended. No holding back, no taking the easy option.

And now I am on this track of thinking, perhaps there may be a third weapon to my advantage. At the end of the Second World War, there came a chance for my mother to become a teacher, needing only to undergo one year of training, as there was such a shortage. On the morning of her interview, three-year-old Judith woke up with scarlet fever. And so the big question arose. Who was to look after her? In those far-off days of the 1940s, it was unthinkable for my father not to turn up at the office but to take charge of a sick child instead.

The inevitable happened. My mother stayed at home. The opportunity never arose again, so she never became a teacher. Perhaps it is of some comfort to her – and she may look upon it as her destiny – that she has produced two daughters for the profession.

If she had indeed turned up for her interview on that fateful day, she might never have got round to having a second baby, being too busy in a classroom somewhere and thus, I would not have been born. A sobering thought.

So I am determined not to be a dutiful daughter for the rest of my life. I am following my inclination to do a little bit of good in this world, safe in the knowledge that my mother is behind me.

Just as she is now, peering into the basin to see if the pudding mix is smooth and creamy enough. Wearing one of Mam's flowery pinnies round my waist, I chat non-stop, while I whisk milk into the eggs and flour. As always, she is eager to know all about the goings-on in Dale House. The names trip off my tongue: how funny Mary is, how odd Penny can be, how I get on so well with Jill and how my room-mate runs off home every Friday night.

Life goes on as usual at home: my mother goes to the office each day, still does the weekly wash, the shopping on a Saturday and then church twice on Sundays – Holy Communion and Evensong, regular as clockwork. And the sparrows still twitter among the branches of the privet in the yard.

My routine is so different, my way of life so changed, everything shared, open and new. I explain how when going to bed, we all know each other's rituals. After queueing for our one and only bathroom, Fran will say a personal goodnight to all her poster idols on her pinboard. I'm told that I take an age to smother my face with moisturising cream and write in my five-year diary. Then there are Jill's rabbits. She checks that the faded, cuddle-worn, cloth creatures are still all present and waiting under her blankets. They have enjoyed delightful seclusion and anonymity for eighteen years, but now their existence is broadcast to the world.

Mam laughs about it, but I can tell that communal living is not to her exacting taste. She's been independent far too long.

We slide the pudding tins into the oven and I start to set the table. Serviettes in their round, chrome holders to the left, glasses of water to the right. Just for now, while at home, I am happy to be playing the kitchen maid. Setting out the knives and forks, I rattle on, telling Mam how on our corridor, there's an unwritten rule that possessions should be lent out and borrowed without complaint. In the world of a tea bag in a mug, my luxury object is a bright yellow china teapot, complete with matching milk jug and sugar bowl. Of course, it had been Judith's when she went to college. As ever, I get the cast-offs.

I am not ungrateful. There are many advantages to being the youngest, as in inheriting teapots, for instance. That brightly coloured china set, the only one on our corridor, has appeared on many occasions, being used whenever anyone's parents come to visit Dale House.

You have to adapt or go under, but I don't voice that to my mother. In fact, I know that I am settling rapidly into communal life. I've heard of plenty of girls my age who have flown back to the home nest. Mam tells me of one, a fellow school pupil of mine, who lasted barely three weeks. Unlike me, an average also-ran, she had always been a clever girl, with a track record of being, 'top of the class'. Whether it was the teaching or the living in such close proximity with others, I will never know. That is probably the reason why St Mag's have had us into schools so quickly in the first term.

Over our dinner of beef, perfectly risen Yorkshire puddings, dishes of buttery veg and jugs full of Mam's excellent gravy, I cheerfully regale tales to Judith and Pete about my early teaching mishaps. I show them that I'm made of sterner stuff. They won't see me flying back home.

Before I know it, all too soon, the week's holiday is over. Arriving at Dale House for the second half of this first autumn term, how easy it is to slip into my new world, dump my bags onto the bed in my room, ask Penny if she's done much to her Education file and pass round a tin of my mother's homemade butterfly cakes. Where now is that domestic scene which I have just left behind? By early evening, it has already faded.

Jill and Pat are writing essays, their desks strewn with piles of open books. Penny is just lowering the needle on her humble turntable to play her precious Glenn Miller and 'Little Brown Jug' for the thousandth time. Mary, her head swathed in a white towel, has washed her hair and smelling powerfully of pink Camay, she pats me as she passes, saying in her familiar flat North-East accent, "Hiya, kidda".

My room-mate's not yet back, late as usual, too involved with her boyfriend back at home. I pop my head round Fran's door to find her furiously trying to rearrange her wardrobe.

"Amelia, would you help me to take this hem up sometime?" I warn her that my stitches are the dog's teeth sort.

Meanwhile, Penny yells from her room next door that she has borrowed my scissors, and I yell back, "When are you going to get a pair of your own?"

She replies that she can't afford them and anyway, she has lent me her copy of Homer's *Odyssey*.

"Oh well." I shrug and lie back on my bed. I close my eyes and sink into the softness of my red tartan rug and dream about supper: a slice of toast with a mug of coffee, flavoured as ever with a spoonful of powdered milk. Oh, yes, and one of Mam's butterfly cakes, sprinkled liberally with icing sugar - a treat!

I am full of contentment.

CHAPTER NINE

～～

NOVEMBER 14TH 1969

ANCIENT AND MODERN

Today it's Jill's birthday. She is all of nineteen years old. You can tell something must be happening, because her bed doesn't look right. The mattress is upside down on top of the sheets and blankets, her corduroy jeans are laid across her chair with the bottoms of the legs all sewn up and the cruellest thing of all, her treasured bunnies are drawing-pinned to the pin board above the bed. It was Penny and Mary's idea and I am ashamed to say that Pat, Fran and I had simply gone along with it. It must be the worst-ever birthday present to come back to after lectures. I secretly hope that Jill will take it in good spirit.

Crouching quietly in her room, we hear her coming

along the corridor. As she opens the door, we see her face fall as she realises the damage. Just in time to save the situation, we leap out, chanting, "Happy birthday to you, happy birthday to you, happy birthday dear Ji-ill, happy birthday to you!"

We fall silent as she stands unsmiling. Then she strides across to the pin board, rescues her rabbits and lays them on the upturned mattress. I am mightily relieved when, with a grin on her face, she picks up Pat's pillow from the opposite bed and begins buffeting Penny and Mary, correctly picking out the perpetrators of the crime. As they retaliate with cushions, the rest of us retreat to safer quarters to let them do battle.

Thinking about the dozen jam tarts and the chocolate cake we clubbed together to buy this morning down in the town makes me feel only slightly better. That should sweeten the bitterness of the earlier horrible surprise.

Back in my room, Fran and I are just getting the birthday tea organised when one of the third years appears at the open door. With a serious expression on her face, she informs us we are wanted down in Miss Robinson's study.

"She's expecting you there in ten minutes' time."

"Just me, or all of us?"

The third year nods. "Everyone from this corridor. So be sharp."

I open my mouth to speak. "And before you ask," she interrupts, "I have no idea why."

Every Hall of Residence houses one or two lecturers to look after the interests of the female students. Although they are legally 'in loco parentis', generally we don't see much of the staff and we are left for the most part to our own devices, without any interference. So to be summoned to an interview is quite an event.

None of us have any idea why we are standing outside Miss Robinson's study, but it's difficult not to look at each other with nervous, even guilty expressions.

Penny, the bravest amongst us, steps forward and knocks on the door. Hearing a firm "Come in", we all troop inside and stand in a single line facing our resident lecturer, who is sitting in an easy chair, surrounded by books. The room is filled with them. They are everywhere, littering the coffee table, in untidy heaps on the floor and filling shelves in glass-fronted cases along the wall. A pile of what looks like handwritten essays lies on a side table next to her, obviously ready to be marked.

I look up at the high corniced ceilings and at a view overlooking the main road from the wide bay window. It feels like a cocoon in here, separate and sheltered, away from the lively antics up and down our corridors: a place to escape to for an academic lecturer, to read, prepare courses and consider the merits of her students' work. It is private and quiet, whereas we must sleep, eat, study and learn together, with only a painted wooden partition to separate us.

Like the rest of Dale House, it feels warm in here, but

in a more muffled, enclosed sort of way. Then I realise we are standing on thick carpet, unlike our clinically smooth lino at our end. A sickly smell of sweet perfume hangs in the air, which reminds me of old ladies. I think of an elderly neighbour we used to have, living next door to us back at home. She was a retired spinster teacher, who would give me, as a small child, biscuits out of round brown tins. Everything in her house was brown and dark: the furniture, the walls, the paintwork. All except for the flowery overall she wore every day.

At this moment, I make a promise to myself that I will not become a sad, spinster teacher, surrounded only by books and living in a brown house. I feel young, younger than my eighteen years. Miss Robinson, I guess, is in her late forties, or maybe early fifties, but then, compared to us mere teenagers, she is ancient.

She looks at us each in turn with piercing, unblinking eyes. Her dark mousy hair, curling untidily and uncombed, manages to enhance her decidedly school ma'am appearance. We lower our direction of gaze like naughty school girls.

What terrible transgression have we committed? Has Jill complained about the treatment she received on her birthday? Childish though it was, would that deserve being hauled in front of a lecturer? To my knowledge, Jill had never left her room. In fact, the pillow-and-cushion battle was still going on when we received the summons. So what else could it be?

After a long uncomfortable silence, Miss Robinson enlightens us.

"Now girls."

She's talking down to us, I think, treating us as if we're back at school.

"I know you like to enjoy yourselves, listen to music and have a joke every now and then."

I glance nervously across at Penny. Does old Robbie have x-ray vision, or maybe there is a spy in the camp?

Then her tone changes. Her voice rises another octave.

"But there is a limit. By ten minutes to eleven at night, we do not expect to hear such goings on as Mr McNulty has done. On several occasions, I might add. Both before and after the half-term vacation."

What 'goings on', I silently wonder? The expressions on the faces of the others reveal they are as puzzled as I am.

"It is unfortunate," she continues, "that students are forced to live in rooms above our caretaker and his family." And here, Miss Robinson takes on her best grammar school teacher attitude. "But one must have Tolerance. Tolerance for our neighbours. Your neighbours happen to live underneath you."

As she pauses for breath, Mary manages to squeeze in, "What exactly has he heard, Miss Robinson?"

The aggrieved lecturer draws in a deep breath and shifts slightly in her chair, to sit up even more erectly. "Bangs, yells, doors clashing, records blazing at full volume. Simply insufferable noise. It will have to stop."

"Well, there are eight of us to use the bathroom every evening," puts in Penny, bravely.

"And no carpet in the corridor," Mary adds.

The rest of us keep our lips closed.

By now, Miss Robinson's nervous system is highly inflamed. "I'm sure you all don't go to bed at once."

Our statements of defence are proving useless.

She stands up, clasps her hands together in front of her and regards us as if we are that wretched Class 3B on a rainy Friday afternoon. It is clear the interview is coming to an end, as we are now issued with our final orders.

"From now on, you use the bathroom earlier, take care in closing doors, turn off all music by ten o'clock at the very latest. And above all…" She pauses. The last word comes out in a menacing whisper. "Tiptoe!"

As we slink out, looking suitably shamefaced but inwardly indignant, the irate Miss Robinson fires the parting shot.

"And I shall be up there at half past ten exactly, to ensure you have carried this out."

Indignant or not, we are left with little choice. It is no use saying didn't she know students normally play loud music and talk until the early hours. Surely, that is half the reason we have chosen to leave home. It is the fault of stupid old College, putting us in rooms above a sensitive caretaker. But I imagine Miss Robinson would only have replied that the most important reason to be there was to train to be good, upstanding teachers of the next generation. And she would have been right, of course. Apart from Penny and Mary pointing out the obvious about bathrooms and carpets, none of us dared to put forward our point of view. We were painfully aware that we were on the losing side.

Nevertheless, it doesn't stop us grumbling amongst ourselves for the rest of the evening. Penny reminds us all that there's been much talk lately of the Government's plan to lower the age of majority.

"So, when it comes down from twenty-one to eighteen," she explains hotly, "we'll all legally be adults."

We realise then that there'll be no signing out, no need to require permission for late night passes and as Mary points out, we'll even be eligible to vote. Sadly, that day has not yet arrived.

It's ten o'clock now and Jill, the last one in the bathroom on our newly drawn up strict rota, pads silently in slippers and dressing gown along the carpetless corridor. Everyone is ready for bed and in their respective rooms. As she passes my door, she peeps in and whispers, "This is most unlike us, isn't it? How are we going to stand it?"

I feel equally glum. "No idea. What's going to happen to our late-night vigils?"

"That's just it. No more laughing and talking till two in the morning."

I snigger as quietly as possible. "We must have been making poor McNulty suffer all these weeks."

Jill grins. "Nasty, old Robbie will be after us for ever more now. Well, better say goodnight. The ancient scarecrow might be down any minute trying to catch us out."

"Jill," I whisper as she closes the door, "how are those rabbits of yours? None the worse for being pinned to the board?"

It is fortunate for me that this friend I have known for only a matter of a few weeks holds no grievances and is not without a great sense of humour.

She winks. "They've survived."

"But more to the point, have you?"

"Give them their due, Penny and Mary did restore my bed to rights," Jill says, as she holds on to the door handle. "But let's put it this way, those jam tarts and that chocolate cake were definitely the best part of the day."

She disappears and I snuggle down with a paperback copy of *Mansfield Park*, the next novel to be read and inwardly digested for my Jane Austen tutorial. I feel more content, now that I know Jill's feelings haven't been permanently scarred for life.

Minutes later, I hold my breath as Robbie's footsteps are heard, as she had warned, exactly on the dot of half past ten, according to my little alarm clock. All is unnaturally quiet: record player silent, lights out, doors closed. I imagine her breathing a sigh of relief and going back to her escape room, to her lonely pile of books and essay marking.

Mr McNulty can be sure of at least one night's peaceful sleep.

CHAPTER TEN

~~~~

DECEMBER 1969

THE FESTIVE FEELING

We have tiptoed our way right through into December and now there's no getting away from it. The festive season is upon us: Christmas themes in Education, nativity plays in RE, decorations put up in the main hall and carol singing in chapel.

Today it's Sunday and late into the afternoon. Unusually no one has gone home this weekend, and somehow all eight of us have managed to squeeze into Mary and Penny's room for coffee. With the curtains not yet drawn, I can see the bare branches of the cherry tree against a sky beginning to turn a velvety shade of navy blue.

Six of us sprawl lazily across the two beds and the two chairs, so that the legal occupiers are relegated to cushions on the floor. Essays are complete and the end of term beckons. We all agree, it's been an exhausting couple of weeks. For a few moments, the only sound that can be heard is that of intermittent slurps of hot tea and coffee and the murmurs of thanks as a tin of digestives is passed around. We have little energy for anything else. Even Penny's turntable is silent, as no one feels in the mood for 'In the Mood'.

During this hiatus of peace, Mary pipes up. She tells us that earlier today she happened to go over to Beechwood House, another Hall of Residence, to borrow a book from someone.

"They've done a wonderful job of decorating their corridor with huge painted figures of the nativity. Somehow, they've even made a model stable. Mind you, I don't know where they got the straw from."

"West Wing have done theirs like Santa's Grotto," says Pat, "with little elves and hanging tinsel and everything".

Penny wonders if we ought to do something festive in our own corridor.

"Well the bad news is," points out Jill, as practical as ever, "there's only a week left before we go down." Apparently, 'going down' is the correct phrase for breaking up for the holidays. We might wear brand new College scarves, but we have already adopted the new language.

"But here's the good news," and she leaps out of the chair and dives into her room. Ten seconds later, she triumphantly produces a white painted branch, festooned with handmade silver paper balls and tissue paper flowers of red and green.

"It's a sort of Christmas tree," she tells us, unnecessarily. "I made it just this afternoon in my Education lecture."

Mary rolls off her cushion on the floor and stands up awkwardly. "That's great, Jill. It's a start. But what can we stand it in?"

With the production of a tree, we are all galvanised into action. Someone finds a large coffee jar, purchased during a wealthy period. We tip the remaining coffee grains into several mugs. Then Mary unearths a sheet of wrapping paper, adorned with fat, cheery Santa Clauses, and winds it round the jar to disguise its origins.

Jill holds the completed Christmas tree carefully. "Now where can we stand it?"

Penny whizzes out into the corridor. "Well, it needs to be out here."

This enthusiasm is infectious. Putting our previous lethargy to one side, we all follow and start making suggestions. Fran decides to run upstairs to ask the third years if they have anything that might do for streamers.

"Why not put the tree here?" I suggest, and move back the curtains hanging at the window at the end of the corridor, just outside Penny's room. The sill is just wide enough to accommodate the coffee jar.

"Look what I've managed to conjure up from our friends above." Fran runs towards us, trailing red and yellow crêpe paper and in her hand, the *pièce de résistance*, two white candles. "We'll make it a real tree, like the German ones and have lighted candles on it instead of fairy lights."

While Jill and Pat drape twisted paper streamers across our room doors, Penny and I try to fasten the candles onto the twigs. "It's no good, Fran. They won't stand up straight. We need some sort of holders. Unless we just balance them on the ledge of the sash, instead of on the tree," says Penny and goes to hunt for something suitable in her junk box she's been collecting for school. Two tin foil plates seem to be the answer and are pressed into shape to act as candle holders.

So now the makeshift tree stands in the middle of the window, with a candle at either side, the flickering lights shining out across the dark College lawns. Yellow and red streamers drape the doors and the white wooden walls of our corridor. We survey our handiwork and all agree that it has brought some much-needed festive spirit into our part of Dale House.

The flurry of activity over, we disperse into our respective rooms to pursue various Sunday evening tasks: washing hair, filing nails, lying on the bed reading, or lying on the bed pretending to read.

After a few minutes, Penny knocks on my door. She wants to show me her latest jumble sale acquisition. This time it's a fur jacket with what looks like a real fox draped around her neck. Its nose and front paws rest on her shoulder and its beady, soulful eyes stare out alarmingly. I wonder in what dreadful manner it had met its death. Horrified, I exclaim, "It's so lifelike!"

"That's because it is, you dumb-cluck. At least it was when it was alive." She fastens some hidden buttons on the edge of the jacket, strokes the creature's nose affectionately and parades in front of the mirror. She eyes first the head and paws side and then the drooping bushy tail at the other.

"How you can wear that, I do not know, Penelope. You could at least have got an artificial one."

"Don't you appreciate, this is the real 1940s thing?" Penny models more furiously than ever. "I paid all of ten and six for this little gem."

I think of all the things a ten-shilling note would buy: at least half a dozen packets of biscuits, probably even chocolate ones. By now I am sitting upright on my bed, leaning comfortably against the wall, my well-thumbed and pencil-marked copy of Victorian poetry tossed aside.

"When are you going to wear this marvellous fox fur, then? The next College Dance?"

All thoughts of when Penny was going to sport this curious piece of apparel are immediately banished from our heads in the ensuing seconds. We are distracted by the sound of heavy footsteps thudding up the cellar stone stairs. Someone has taken the quickest way in via our basement, which, like the front door, remains unlocked until ten thirty.

A voice yells, "You're on fire!"

Penny and I hurtle out into the corridor. Hearing the shouting and commotion, the others open their three doors simultaneously.

Lo and behold, there are bright red, glowing flames at the end window. At once we see that one of our festive Christmas candles has toppled from its tin foil holder onto an unsuspecting, upturned mop. Part of the cleaner's equipment, it normally leans innocently in the corner next to a long broom and a tin bucket. Now the head of the mop is burning merrily.

Without thinking of the consequences, Penny grabs the mop and dashes down the corridor, holding the handle at arm's length as if making an assault on a medieval castle wall. The smoke billows into each of our four open rooms as she charges down in knight errant style to the bathroom. The offending mop head is submerged into the sink and drowned, sizzling under the cold tap. The fumes make our eyes water and our rooms smell foul.

Once we recover from the shock, the other candle is duly blown out for safety's sake. Now, we all collapse into fits of relieved laughter, weakly leaning against the corridor walls, wiping our eyes and make desperate attempts not to think of smouldering mop heads.

Eventually, normality is resumed and we turn to the girl who raised the alarm, to ask her side of the story.

"Well, I was sitting in our common room," explains our saviour of the moment, "And I'd just got up to draw the curtains, when I noticed a sort of flickering at your gable end window. It didn't look like a steady light bulb, so, I dashed straight outside to make sure. Good thing I did. As I came up those stairs, I could smell it."

"And we never noticed a thing," says Penny, grimly. "I suppose because we all had our doors shut."

"Goodness knows what might have happened if you hadn't come over," adds Mary with dramatic gloom.

"The whole mop might have gone up then," Fran blurts out and we all dissolve into fits of laughter again.

Perhaps it is fortunate that for now, we can only see the funny side. None of us gives a thought to the fact that the curtains were perilously close to catching fire. And also, our living quarters are divided by wooden panels, no doubt highly combustible. It might have been more than just the cleaning equipment that was burnt to a crisp.

"Here," I interrupt the guffaws coming from the others. "What's the cleaner going to say, when she sees she's minus one functioning mop?"

Then Jill reminds us about the inevitable wrath of Miss Robinson. By the look on everyone's face, no one else has given this a thought.

Sure enough, less than ten minutes later, the news, or rather the tell-tale fumes, have reached our long-suffering resident lecturer. For the second time this term, we stand in her room like school girls, admittedly this time looking suitably ashamed. We endure a great deal of general hauling over the coals and reminders that after all, we are hoping to become professional teachers in charge of young children and there we are, behaving like irresponsible first-year juniors.

Privately, I think that we are simply irresponsible first-year students, not yet fit to be let loose on the world. Definitely not fit to be left in charge of a lighted candle, anyway.

Old Robbie continues with more 'I'm surprised at you' phrases, until somehow Penny and I are elected to purchase one mop head, first thing in the morning.

Gazing at the household section in Woolworth's, we have never seen such a range of dusters, polish and scrubbing brushes. To our amazement, one of the counter displays is completely dedicated to mop heads in a variety of sizes. We must rack our brains to remember exactly what our own mop head looked like before we carelessly set it on fire. It is with a great deal of courage and resilience that we take our choice to a salesgirl, hand over the collected money, while resisting the urge to completely double up, over the statement, "We would like to buy this mop head, please".

The replacement is dutifully presented to the cleaner, after a communal apology from all eight of our guilty party. I have a feeling she completely forgives us, as she looked secretly pleased to acquire a brand-new mop, whatever the means.

Two days later, the seriousness of the situation has

still not sunk into our heads. From our point of view, we had only been trying to make our place of abode more Christmassy. And what is more Christmassy than lit candles, shining out into the darkness of the night? The fact that the cleaner's mop, brush and bucket happened to be in the corner was merely unfortunate. But perhaps dear old Robbie had a point. I suppose the whole candle idea was irresponsible.

The festive feeling has died a quick death after that fateful evening. When we got back from our trip to Woollies, the others had torn down the streamers and Jill had taken back possession of her white painted tree. We have to make do with a few Christmas cards stuck on to our pin boards.

I think the only real lesson we learnt from the incident was, for the sake of our sanity, never to mention again the words 'mop head'.

My first term at College is finally at an end. We all feel as if we have achieved a milestone. Almost every subject has been approached from the point of view of teaching young children. We have sung and drawn and painted and danced and climbed up ropes in the gym. We have begun Mathematics from its most basic start and called it Number, with a capital N. We've begun the study of childhood, to understand how young minds learn, under the heading Education, with a capital E. We have found joy in our own main subjects and most importantly, we survived three weeks in school, standing in front of a class and hearing our own voices.

There will be more to come. Much more. I know the surface has barely been scratched.

We are tired. It feels only right that the Christmas spirit should now be shared at home.

It's the very last evening before we are due to 'go down', or begin our 'vacation': another new word in our vocabulary. We are ready for the mass exodus. Our packed suitcases stand waiting next to bags full of work, including something called a 'Home and School file', which none of us is looking forward to. The lights are out much earlier than usual, even before our enforced ten thirty.

This turns out to be fortunate. During what seems to be the middle of the night, from the undercover warmth of the blankets, I gradually become conscious of the sound of far-away singing and yet, strangely, now not so far away. In fact, these angelic voices seem to be getting nearer. I realise they are not outside, but here, in Dale House. The words become clearer and I hear distinctly the melody and the words of 'Once in Royal David's City'.

I imagine there are not just half a dozen singers, but a great number. The voices begin to filter along our corridor. Through our slightly open door, I can see a lantern being carried on a pole, exactly like those seen on Christmas cards. Singing as they go, they move to the end of the corridor, to stand in a group, until they reach the end of the carol, '*And he leads his children on, To the place where he is gone*'. Then they make their way out of the house and down the cellar stairs with 'Silent Night'. We jump out of bed to look out of the window to catch a glimpse of the moving crowd of carol singers led by their lamp swinging in the inky darkness, their voices fading away into the distance.

I find out later, that it's a well-kept secret of St Mag's College. No word must be breathed to any first-year student about this annual tradition, which takes place on the last morning of the Christmas term, carried out by second and third years. Even our little group of friends who live on the floor above us have kept quiet. It must be a complete surprise. And it was. We have discovered one more piece of festive spirit: one which none of us will ever forget.

And we will do the same when our turn comes. Next year, we will gather under the horse chestnut tree in the main College grounds at five o'clock in the morning. We will make our way around each Hall of Residence, singing our hearts out in our sweetest voices to the unsuspecting new students. We will bring a lump to each throat and a tear to each eye.

As someone says as we gather in our dressing gowns, "I was dreaming I was in heaven and the angels were singing. Then I woke up and I thought it was true".

CHAPTER ELEVEN

~~~

JANUARY 1970

HOMEMADE CAKE
AND FISH AND CHIPS

"Let's stop for a quick coffee," Judith suggests. "Look. Services one mile."

Pete, my good-natured brother-in-law, duly turns up the slip road off the motorway and without any trouble, parks in one of the many empty spaces outside a small cafe.

The traffic here in the north is lighter than the busy roads I hear about nearer London. Not everyone in County Durham and Yorkshire owns a car. Nearly everyone I know relies on the bus service to get back to College. I have the luxury of throwing my luggage into Pete's boot.

The new motorway is a whizz at making our journey shorter. There are still quite a few roundabouts though on the old stretches of the A1, and that's where the queues are. But we don't mind, as the heater blows out warm air and Judith passes round a tube of fruit gums. We laugh when once again I get the green one, her least favourite. When I was little, she would put it on top so that when she offered them to me, I would have to choose it. I'm a lot wiser now, all round.

We step out onto the tarmac and stretch our legs. Not having grown up in a car-owning household, it always feels like a treat to be driven along, free as a bird and deciding for yourself where you want to stop, so we make the most of every trip.

Waiting for the next bus in the cold and the rain has featured heavily in my life up to now. To visit my grandmother involves two bus rides from home with a long wait for the right connection. I remember when I was about five or six years old waiting with my mother in the dark under a street lamp that made all our clothes look purple. To keep me warm, Mam wrapped me close to her in the ample folds of her Sunday best coat, and it felt like an age before the next bus turned up, belching out diesel fumes and its passengers peering out of steamy windows.

Now that Judith and Pete have their own car, I feel we are at last entering the modern age, without the need for long, uncomfortable bus journeys.

After our coffee, we linger outside to breathe in the chilly fresh air and gaze across the countryside, lit up by a wintry afternoon sun. The view stretches for miles across to the distant hills. But this part of Yorkshire is flying terrain, flat and windswept.

Above us, a glider climbs silently in a cold, blue sky. How often have we left home in damp, coastal mist or pouring rain, only to see the sun break out as we catch our first glimpse of the dales? It is becoming almost a catchphrase in our family, 'It's always fine at Bishopsfield'.

The Christmas vacation has done me good.

I finished the dreaded 'Home and School' file with the aid of a few borrowed books. Courtesy of Mam, I have additions to my limited wardrobe. She bought me two skirts at her local dress shop and then acted as seamstress by sewing up the hems to turn them into fashionable minis. I know she was quite proud of herself, as one of them had box pleats, particularly difficult to do.

There were the usual visits to all the various members of the family to exchange Christmas presents. My grandmother loved the miniature chest of drawers containing matches I picked up on the market last term. At least, I think she liked it, as she placed it on the mantelpiece in the front room at once.

And of course, there was the usual wonderful home cooking. In the boot of Pete's car sits a precious cake tin, the contents of which no doubt will be demolished this very evening.

About an hour later, we arrive in Bishopsfield, which is living up to its reputation of enjoying fine weather in the wintry sunshine. Pete turns off the road in the centre of town to drive up a narrow lane. We pass a picturesque building made up of two or three old cottages, now made into one residence for students, aptly and simply named 'Cottages'. Every time I pass it, I think it would not look out of place on the front of a box of chocolates or would make an absorbing thousand-piece jigsaw. Its lawn slopes down towards the pavement and a gravel path winds up to the front door with its lattice-work porch. There should definitely be roses growing around it in the summer. It is here that my new friend Alison lives and she's told me about its cosy rooms, uneven floors and her tiny square window, looking out onto the side garden. Like a ritual, each time we return, I point it out to Judith and Pete and without fail, they admire its attractions. Alison, we agree, is one of the lucky ones. But I am not disappointed at my own Hall of Residence and I sit up eagerly, looking forward to setting eyes once again on Dale House.

After Cottages we drive along a tree-lined avenue, where the view to our right opens up onto a huge, sweeping lawn in front of College. Even in winter, I still think it is the most beautiful sight. I have seen nothing like it in my own home town, which has three working pits and rows of terraced red-brick houses. There, trees are sparse and mostly stunted by the winds. Here, I feel I am arriving at a country mansion on the edge of town.

At the end of the line of trees and just past the main College drive, Pete turns into the side road to park next to Dale House. He carries my case, not through the front door as he did last September but through the cellar in the basement which is now our usual entrance. The stairs leading up to my corridor run surprisingly and abruptly from a wall, so that one is forced to step onto the bottom stair over the side of the staircase. The reason for this is a puzzle we can never work out. Obviously, the building has been changed over the years. Walls built to create new rooms, stairs running into a dead end – all were part of the charm of the rambling old house.

The beginning of this term feels very different from the last; I am returning to familiar ground, familiar faces. Instead of a blank pinboard next to my bed, it's already plastered with posters and magazine cut-outs: a picture of a sunset, another of a huge wave crashing over the black and white lighthouse at the end of the pier at home and a small, discreet one of Dudley Moore from the *Radio Times*. It's his dark, arching eyebrows that I find so irresistible.

And waiting on one of my shelves is a jar half full of instant coffee. I dash upstairs for the kettle as without the luxury of a kitchen, we must share a tiny one with the third years on the floor above. Sitting on my tartan bedspread and warming cold hands around mugs of hot drinks, Judith and Pete indulge in a little reminiscing about their own college days, when they'd first met: dancing into the early hours and walking along the riverbank on a Sunday afternoon.

Was this going to be the story of my life? I have always followed in my sister's footsteps, dutifully passing the eleven-plus exam and going to the same girls' grammar school. However there are so many years between us that as soon as I reached one stage of my education, Judith had always left for the next one.

And now that I have managed it into the first year of College, she is already married and teaching. So of course, this too I feel I am destined to follow. At some point during my three years here, I will meet the love of my life, just as Judith did. That's part of my unspoken plan.

I once made a list of attributes that my prospective partner should possess. He had to like playing the piano, walking in the countryside and have the ability to make me laugh, though not all at the same time. Crucially, I insisted I would recognise him by his faded corduroy jacket with leather patches at the elbow. Fran, who was interrogating me at the time, could not imagine where I had picked up this idea, and I could not enlighten her. This picture was firmly set in my imagination. I attested that I would never marry, unless someone who fitted this description walked into my life. Fran replied that I was going to be extremely hard to please. In fact, too choosy by half.

Well, I have reached my second term and so far no one has come my way, apart from the unfortunate RAF chap, who definitely did not wear a corduroy jacket. There again, he never made me laugh. But still, I remind myself as I cheerily wave goodbye to Judith and Pete, it's early days yet.

I run back up the stairs, take the lid off Mam's cake tin and pass the goodies round.

A week later and with no sign of either my room-mate or Fran's, we discover that neither of them will be returning at all. We think they must have been so wrapped up with being engaged that college life somehow passed them by. No longer was teaching of any importance to them. They sent letters to Fran and me by way of a farewell, but my instinct tells me that there is little chance of us ever seeing them again.

I decide that won't be my fate. Why should a boyfriend, should I ever find one, spoil my career? No, getting married comes afterwards; training to teach first.

Fran has moved from her room opposite into mine. She has an unenviable reputation for being late handing in essays and I am usually a 'just in time' sort of student, so we spend our evenings trying desperately to keep up with our timetable of work.

Our second goal is not to eat too many bags of chips.

Because of the sometimes lamentable state of College's churned-out meals, the menu becomes so predictable. If it's Tuesday, it must be rubbery beefburgers and soggy green beans. There's often someone zooming down into town straight after tea to the fish shop with gigantic orders. It's not unusual for a student with a purse bulging full of collected change to ask for "fish and chips ten times and one with no vinegar". This last one is for me. The others curse and grumble, but I insist on having mine wrapped separately, vinegar-less.

We have differences of opinion about fish and chip language too. If I'm giving in the order, I ask for ten 'lots' without stating what it is I want ten 'lots' of. I declare that that's what people say in the North-East. If one of the Yorkshire folk go, it will be so many 'times'. Then perhaps, with 'scraps', which means all the little bits of left-over batter dropped over the chips. I simply call that 'batter'.

Quite often, the shop assistants don't understand what I am talking about. In the baker's, if you ask for buns, you are given little fairy cakes. I've learned you have to be specific here and say 'bread buns', whereas for me, little cakes are just called, well, little cakes.

Then, for the messenger who is sent down for the fish and chip order, there is the change to consider. She has to get it exactly right. We are the student equivalent of paupers. Last term, we managed to persuade a girl living at the other end of Dale House, who is very dithery and gullible, to go one rainy night, when no one else would. She bought a plastic carrier bag with the change. It was all hell and damnation when she got back. Our money is precious: we have precious little to see us through the term. Needless to say, we've never bothered to send her for fish and chips again. Perhaps it served us right. We should run our own messages.

With the money situation, I reckon I am one of the lucky ones. The fact that my mother is a widow on a modest income means that I am entitled to a full grant. Even so, my fifty-four pounds for the term has to be carefully eked out over about twelve weeks. The princely sum of three or four pounds can be withdrawn on a Monday. With that, I can buy biscuits and shampoo, a poetry book for school, maybe entry into the Saturday night dance and the odd bag of chips. Anything left over has to be put towards clothes and shoes. Although my Mam, with what little she has, still sends me something extra when she can.

Fran, on the other hand, has no grant at all. Her father is in the fortunate position of being managing director of a factory and so she is reliant upon donations from her parents. They seem to have a happy-go-lucky approach to their daughter's finances, adopting an ad hoc arrangement. It's a case of Fran getting to the bottom of her bank account and having to beg for funds.

Once she wrote to them in desperation. She opened the answering letter in high anticipation and pulled out a ten-shilling note. She looked at me in silent disgust.

It seems that those who have money do not wish to part with it, whereas the generous are often those who have little.

CHAPTER TWELVE

~~~

THE LAST FIRE DRILL

This morning early, although it seems like the middle of the night, we are rudely awakened by the clanging of the fire bell. A bleary-eyed glance at my alarm clock tells me it's five o'clock on the dot. With the incessant ringing at full volume and reverberating in my ears, I fling back the warm sheets and blankets.

'Not again,' I mutter.

Somewhere under the bed is a pair of shoes to shove my feet into and my coat hangs ready on the hook behind the door. By now we are well versed in the procedure and wise to the fact that shoes and coats should be kept handy, just in case. I manage both without fastening either laces or buttons.

As if to teach us a lesson after the infamous 'mop-head incident' at Christmas, it seems we have had an endless number of drills since the beginning of term. Although there happens to be a fire escape contraption outside our corridor window, strangely we have never been given the chance to try it out. That would be at least something exciting to be woken up for. I imagine it's been there since the year dot and doesn't even work. It looks slightly on the rusty side.

Instead, a strict ritual must be obeyed: firstly, leave curtains open, 'to facilitate the entry of a fireman through a window'. Next, the doors must be left wide open, so that the appointed student 'fire warden' from each corridor can check no one is left behind in the rooms. After ensuring all have vacated the premises, so our printed sheet of instructions tells us, the warden has to close the doors on her way out.

Whether we would remember all that opening and closing of curtains and doors, if ever there is smoke pouring along the corridor at two in the morning, is another matter entirely. What I do recall clearly is the panic that ensued when real flames were burning up our mop head at Christmas. Doors and curtains were the last thing on our minds then.

Appointed warden Penny, who had been compelled by the rest of us to 'volunteer', ushers everyone out, correctly closing the doors behind her.

"How many times do we have to suffer this?" she hisses through clenched teeth. "Let's get it right this time for goodness sake, so we don't have to bother with any more of these wretched drills!"

Our emergency exit is down the cellar stairs with a leap at the bottom over the side, where the stairs end abruptly into a wall. Then it's through the laundry, past the spin dryers, out of the door and across the little yard to congregate 'in orderly fashion' under the cherry tree on the side road.

As we clatter down the stone steps to the cellar exit, passing the half-landing window, I mentally note that I can't see anything outside for what seems to be ...smoke.

'My God!' I think. 'It's really happened. These drills aren't for nothing. All that work I've done on my Education file. Now it's all going to be destroyed,' I gasp. 'I could have picked up a bag full of work and saved it.'

But of course, that was another of the cardinal rules, 'Do not waste precious time by stopping to collect any of your possessions'.

These desperate thoughts whizz through my head in the space of a few seconds.

We emerge into the grey light of early morning and stand shivering in our almost orderly lines, the bell still clanging away inside. The abrasive sound cuts through the stillness of the cold, January air as I pull my coat around me more tightly. Some of the girls have simply donned thin, nylon dressing gowns and fluffy slippers. The assembled crowd looks like a queue for some sort of peculiarly subdued fancy dress party.

I slowly realise that we can see neither College nor Miss Pringle's house only a few yards away. There's no sign of the fire brigade yet. How long will it take to get here? Dale House is going to go up in flames at this rate.

I look up to scan the windows. Just where did the fire start? At least, I think with some relief, this time it's none of our doing.

Finally, a feeling of slight dampness gets to me.

"Foggy morning, ladies," smiles Miss Robinson and she proceeds to count heads.

~~~

CHAPTER THIRTEEN

BIRTHDAY TOAST

"Happy birthday to you, happy birthday to you, happy birthday dear Fra-an, happy birthday to you!"

I pull back the curtains. The sun pours into our room, lighting up piles of books and files scattered across the floor. On the table lies an opened packet of thin white sliced bread, plus several coffee-stained mugs and unwashed spoons.

"What a sight to wake up to," I groan. It's obvious that some order must be restored by someone and I realise it will have to be me. Fran seems to be in a permanent state of oblivion to any kind of disorganised mess. After several heavy bounces on the edge the mattress, I resort to flinging back her blankets and manage to drag her from her slumber. She sits up in bed and scrapes back her long brown hair with her hands, without any attempt to brush out the tangles.

With a flourish, I present to the birthday girl a piece of toast smeared thickly with marmalade. After the episode with Jill last term, the members of our corridor made a unanimous decision to abandon the sewn-up trousers and apple-pie bed idea.

Fran rewards me with a slight smile and then a huge yawn.

"Have you been over to breakfast to bring that just for me?"

"Well. I didn't go all the way over to the dining hall just to bring you one measly slice of toast," I say ungraciously. "I did happen to have my own breakfast while I was there."

"Any post yet?"

"There was nothing when I passed the pigeonholes. Expecting piles of cards, are you?" I toss a bright yellow envelope in her direction. "Sorry, I nearly forgot. At least there's one from me."

As if on cue, Jill, Pat and Penny appear at the open door, singing at the tops of their voices.

"Be careful, Mr McNulty might still be snoozing in bed below," I say with mock gravity.

Penny waves her hand as if to sweep away the problem. "Oh, he's had peace since half past ten last night. It's time he was up getting on with his caretaking." She sits down heavily at the end of Fran's bed. "How's the birthday girl? You've got marmalade on your nose, by the way."

"Great, apart from having sticky fingers and crumbs in my bed, I'm just waiting for all these presents I'm supposed to get on the day I turn nineteen."

"And what presents might that be?" asks Jill. "I never got any."

Pat changes the subject deftly. "More importantly and much more pressing, I'm in school tomorrow and I need some art ideas for my five and six-year-olds."

All eyes turn towards her. We can hear the desperation in her voice.

"Lesson plans have to be handed in today."

Penny puts on an encouraging face. "Who's your tutor, Pascoe? Oh, you've got to have something really special for him." Then forgetting to be positive, she adds, "Anyway, it's not Art, it's Creative Activities."

Pat nods and says with her own bizarre kind of logic, "Well, I've got the main creative bit. It's the activities I need." She produces a file and starts flicking over the pages. "I've got no imagination, that's my trouble."

Now it's Jill's turn to try to be reassuring. "Yes, you have. Everybody has."

"Being creative is not separate from activities, you ignoramus," says Penny. She raises her eyes to the ceiling. "All the activities are supposed to *be* creative."

Pat sits slumped at our study table, file in front of her, chin in hands.

"But it's when one kid says, 'I'm finished. *Now* what do I do?' And I say, 'Put some more blue in the sky,' or 'Cut another shape out,' and then they're back thirty seconds later saying, 'I'm finished. What do I do *now*?' And all the scissors are being used and there's no more paper left and everywhere is chaos and you've got another half hour to go before playtime. That's when I feel like crying."

We all look round at each other in common sympathy. The problem Pat just described has probably happened to us all at some point. I would say that every young teacher with ideas and theories in her head but no experience in her defence feels this sense of helpless desperation. One minute the busy class is humming beautifully, creating marvellously. The next minute, half a dozen children have delivered their final flourish and are waving soggy, wet paintings in your face and daubing sticky finger marks on their faces and their neighbours'. They can't do anything clean, like read a book. Besides, there's not a clear surface to be seen in the classroom, everything in sight is covered in newspaper to protect the desk tops from tipped up paint pots and blobs of glue. And so the gleeful group are sent to the cloakroom. This is often sited yards away down a corridor, where you hope they will wash their hands without causing a flood or using up all the paper towels in the dispenser, which were meant to last until the end of the week, or scatter the soggy ones far and wide across the floor, thus incurring the wrath of the caretaker at half past three. I emphasise that this is the young student teacher's plight. No one has yet told us the intricate rules of practical organisation. We are learning these along the way.

"Look," says Jill, calming the situation with some common sense, "you don't have all thirty of them doing sticky and painty things at once. Just organise two groups for sticking and painting and the others doing some construction or cutting out."

Pat's face brightens up as she listens to these words of wisdom.

The rest of us listen as attentively as her five-year olds as Jill continues. Fran has even forgotten about eating her toast. "Then as soon as the first ones are finished, have a place ready to leave their pictures to dry."

Pat opens her mouth to ask the next question, but before she has time to voice it, Jill is ready with the answer. "Those children can go on to the other clean activity, or simply crayon a picture."

Pat's eyes light up.

"Why didn't Pascoe tell us that?"

"Because for years he's been teaching students instead of infants," Penny says ruefully. "How come you've learned the remedy, Jill, anyway?"

"Found out on my Teaching Practice. Learnt the hard way." The look in her eyes tells the whole story.

Fran, still holding on to her second half slice of birthday toast, slides out of bed and passes the marmalade mound to Pat. "Here, reckon you need that more than I do," she grins, and we all breathe a sigh of relief.

Crisis averted.

CHAPTER FOURTEEN

~~~~

NO BATS IN THE BELFRY

"'Collect fungi,' it says here, 'but don't poison yourself at lunch time – make sure you wash your hands before eating'."

"Do they think we're five years old?" Fran comments.

The two of us have been press-ganged into collecting the latest handouts and I'm reading our instructions aloud as we saunter along the path from College, through the White Gates and along by Dale House. The cherry tree under our window is in delicate white blossom. Tiny petals are fluttering everywhere like snowflakes and gathering in soft heaps at the side of the road, with their perfume carried along in the mild, early spring air. That now familiar continual cooing of woodpigeons from the high trees in the Principal's garden transports me for a moment back to my interview day. Around us I hear the voices of students talking, discussing, laughing. Like us, they dawdle from lectures back to Halls, their arms full of books and files bursting with notes. It's almost a year ago now since, on that first visit, while surveying a similar scene, I was enchanted by the spell woven by St Mag's. Now I understand its magic.

Fran and I turn in at the side gate, through our customary cellar door and up the flight of stairs leading to our corridor. The latest Education hand-out prompts much discussion. The other girls are back from lectures before us and gathered in Penny's room, completely oblivious to the kettle steaming away merrily to itself on the lino floor in the corridor next to our one and only plug.

As I pass, I flick off the switch. "Kettle's boiling its bottom off," I call through the open door.

I watch Mary while she hurls several spoonfuls of coffee into some mugs, tips in the obligatory, powdered milk and goes to retrieve the kettle through the steamy haze.

"Well, ladies, it's Moreton again next week," I announce, now that coffee is organised. Groans ensue.

"What happy experience awaits us this time?" asks Jill.

"Well, it says here," I read aloud from the printed sheet, "'A visit to the market square to observe the buildings including the church, a study of the fields around the village, taking extra care NOT TO DISTURB

THE DRY STONE WALLS, noting vegetation, stock etc, etc'."

"Oh Lord, just what I need," moans Penny. "How many miles this time, do you reckon?"

We all remember a previous task which involved trekking along the river bank and arriving back at the college bus footsore and weary.

"Can't be worse than last time," I say, in a consoling sort of way. "Oh, and I forgot to mention, you have to make notes as you go along," I add cheerfully.

"What has that got to do with teaching kids in a class, I wonder?" asks Pat.

Mary gives me a knowing glance as she hands out scalding mugs of coffee. As far as teacher training goes, Pat still seems to be in the dark.

On a bright but breezy Monday morning, we gather in Moreton market square for an Education outing, as our handout indicated last week. "I'm in Group Two with you, Alison," I whisper at the back of a huddle of students.

When I told her the other day how lucky she was to live in the picture-perfect Cottages, she replied that it was far too quiet over there. That made me think that perhaps she is secretly envious of our more boisterous crowd in Dale House. In any case, she explains, it may be picturesque, but it's certainly not practical.

I do remember once, one of the third years who lives

there producing her room key. It was made from thick metal, at least six inches in length and weighed down her bag considerably. It looked like the latest find from an archaeological dig. Apparently, her room leads straight out into the garden and so has to be locked. Alison says that they are often bothered with rumours of prowlers looking in through the old sash windows, although she's never actually seen one herself. I suppose Dale House sounds to her a much more cheerful option.

Today Alison seems pleased that we are to be together for our field study. However, I discover she has an ulterior motive. "Great! We can collaborate on notes," she says.

I try to sound helpful. "Well, the tour round church won't be a problem. I do know the difference between a pew and a pulpit."

"But do you know anything about stock or vegetation for the field bit later on? I haven't got a flipping clue," she hisses.

I have to admit to my lack of expertise in that direction. "All I recognise are daisies and dandelions. Oh, and clover," I reply, revealing the full extent of my wild flower knowledge, having spent my childhood playing in yards, back streets and on the beach.

Alison was not impressed. "That's not vegetation."

"What is then?"

"Things like oats and beans and barley, I think."

I pull a face. "Well I know even less about them. Do beans grow in a field?"

As my voice rises, all eyes are turned towards us. Miss Flowerdew, our Education lecturer, aptly named as she is College's specialist in all things environmental, speaks in her most haughty manner.

"Would the ladies at the back please be quiet and pay attention?"

A frail-looking figure, she is swamped by her usual attire of tartan pleated skirt with a twin set of jumper and buttoned-up cardigan. Her voice comes out in a strangled squeak. This happens whenever she is enraged, which is usually towards the end of every Education lecture, when her patience is sorely tried by inattentive students.

To suppress our giggles, Alison and I consider our sensible lace-up shoes for the next thirty seconds. Before we recover from the embarrassment, the order is given that everyone in Group Two must first proceed to the church, as our field study is not until the afternoon session.

Alison and I heave a sigh of relief. A tramp around looking for oats and beans and barley can wait. Far more attractive is the safety of the church, a much more familiar environment to me. Plus, it's a lot less muddy than open fields.

Mr Taylor, our Religious Education lecturer, is standing by ready to escort us, jangling the church keys in one hand and in the other gripping his ancient, well-worn briefcase, which is bulging with no doubt informative but deadly boring notes.

"That's us." Alison digs me in the ribs.

We have to move quickly to catch up with the rest of the group, already halfway across the market square: willing, attentive students, notebooks in one hand, pencils poised at the ready. Perhaps they will all end up as headmistresses, or at least better teachers than I can become.

Mr Taylor has his own personal little flock around him, ready to pop the most vital question. Naturally, the answer will be integral to one of the central themes in their next Teaching Practice. They move at speed, sticking closely to the tall, lean figure of our leader, who is striding across to the corner of the square, through the iron gates and up the path between the gravestones, finally halting outside the wooden door of the church, the group only inches behind.

Alison and I hurry after them, taking a few much-needed breaths when we arrive, once again at the back, only managing to catch the last snippets of Mr Taylor's diatribe.

"...Norman, as of course it was largely built during the fourteenth century. Inside ladies, please notice Father Time and also the cherub blowing bubbles." He looks meaningfully around his students while Alison and I hide our faces behind our notebooks, trying to stifle the laughter.

"Who was Norman, for goodness sake?" I whisper.

"And a cherub blowing bubbles?" Alison blurts out,

causing both of us to finally lose the battle in remaining serious.

We try our best to return to straight faces, putting on the guise of well-intentioned students as we step inside the cool, quiet church. Our footsteps and subdued voices echo around the lofty stone pillars as we traipse up and down the aisles, examine the wooden, carved pews, the brass plaques in the nave and search for the cherub blowing bubbles. In silence we crane our necks to gaze at the Victorian stained-glass windows, which are letting in shafts of spring sunshine through colours of brilliant blues and reds.

This is where I spent a good deal of my younger years. Not exactly in this very church, but in my own, hardly a stone's throw from the house where I was born and grew up. For years it has been second nature to me to let my eyes roam around these centuries-old buildings while enduring endless sermons. The windows and the patterns in stone work have afforded me hours of entertainment.

Sunday was all about church. Morning communion, Sunday school in the afternoon, and later it would be a more grown-up Bible class. Even later there was Sunday School teaching to be done in preparation for College and then, to round off the day, Evensong. I succumbed to it all.

As a teenager, Judith once rebelled. She announced to Mam after dinner one Sunday that she didn't think she would bother going to church that evening. Our mother didn't argue, she didn't rant and rave. She simply said quietly that if that were the case, she would expect to find her in bed on our return. I remember coming back home from church with Mam and indeed, my sister was tucked up and with the light out. I don't think she ever tried that again.

Never being quite the rebellious sort, I have, however, always been up for some fun and am happy to seek any humour that might be extracted from a situation, such as today, standing in Moreton parish church.

"Now ladies," announces our esteemed lecturer, after handing round sheaves of typed notes from his battered briefcase. From the look of the curled-up edges of the papers, no doubt generations of students before us have received much the same. He presses his palms together and gives us one of his gleaming-eyed looks.

"Now that we have seen the main body of the church, perhaps the *stout-hearted* amongst you" – here he shoots a piercing glance towards the back of the group where Alison and I are lurking – "those with courage and stamina, may like a peep up into the belfry." He makes this sound like the highlight of the morning, if not the whole day, not to be missed.

Everyone looks shiftily at each other. The faithful, ardent ones at the front nod eagerly, out of thirst for knowledge and loyalty to their tutor. The middle, weary lot, shake their heads. They are thinking, no doubt, of all those narrow, stone steps with nothing but spiders and bats to endure for all their monumental effort. Meanwhile, Alison and I raise our hands with new enthusiasm, out of thirst for adventure and anything for a laugh.

Five minutes later, while the middle, probably sensible lot escape outside to the sun and relative safety among the cheery gravestones, the earnest and the jolly ones follow in the wake of Mr Taylor and his bulging briefcase to climb dozens of winding steps.

We enter the musty, dark belfry, our eyes blinking, adjusting to the gloom, while our leader pauses for breath after mounting the spiral staircase, ascending the final, rickety, almost vertical ladder and finally shouldering open the wooden trapdoor at the top.

We examine the bells, several centuries old and, on tiptoe, peep out of slit windows to view the market square far down below. It looks like a toy town with miniature figures scurrying in and out of the shops and the café, an ideal Yorkshire country village, its buildings perfectly placed where life is ordered and the way it ought to be.

On the inside, disappointingly, there is no sign of a bat or even a solitary spider scuttling along the dusty floorboards, although several cobwebs in the corners give away their presence. All the indoor wildlife must have disappeared into cracks and crevices when they heard us stampede upon their territory.

At last, all facts expounded, comes the welcome, "Down we go." The ever-cheerful Mr Taylor ushers us carefully towards the hatch in the floor, like a shepherd guiding his sheep. He instructs us unnecessarily in how to safely descend backwards down the creaky wooden ladder. One or two of the girls are a little hesitant in beginning the downward journey and grip fiercely onto the rungs. I have no fear of heights and relish the challenge. I smile broadly at Alison, who is following me, to let her know how much fun this is.

Gingerly we feel our way down in the semi-darkness, winding round and round, patting the stone wall as we go. After each student is safely on terra firma at the back of the church, Mr Taylor joins us at last and turns the long iron key in the little wooden door behind us. Once outside, he slams shut and locks the heavy main door with another even bigger key, almost twice the size of the one for Cottages.

We meet the rest of the group outside in the glaring sunshine. Full of chatter about our excursion into the gloomy heights, we saunter along the path between the graves towards the big wrought iron gates at the end of the churchyard. This time Mr Taylor is bringing up the rear, in deep conversation with the extra-eager girls who always yearn for more information.

Then everyone stops as one body when he lets out a loud, "Oh no! You're right, so I have!"

At once, he turns on his heel and strides purposefully back up the path towards the church door.

"Where's he off to now?" I ask one of his ardent admirers.

"Back up the belfry to get his briefcase," she says.

~~~

CHAPTER FIFTEEN

MAY 1970

THAT'S WHAT FRIENDS ARE FOR

It's the summer term. Now the six of us in our corridor feel as though we have known one another all our lives and College will go on for ever. Our comradeship is firmly cemented: we gel together as one group or in pairs or even threes, but certainly some friendships seem stronger than others. Jill, who shares with Pat, seems to have an affinity with me. She and I both have, to different degrees, an obtuse nature. Sometimes on Saturday nights we both stay in and refuse to go to the weekly dance because neither of us can face the 'cattle market' as it is dubbed. Then when the fancy takes us, we go along with the others and happily bob about to the music around our handbags, all the while trying to ignore the line of males along the edge of the hall.

When we first arrived last September, we discovered we were the only girls to wear pyjamas in bed, and stoutly declared that they were the most comfortable nightwear. However, now it's summer, Jill and I have succumbed and have come back after the Easter holidays with nighties: one more step away from childhood.

"Which just goes to show," Jill declares the first night back while queueing up at our one bathroom for teeth cleaning, "what strength of character Amelia and I have, to change our minds, considering all the mockery poured upon us!"

Nothing more is said about the matter.

I might be away from home and trying my best to be grown up, but in some ways I still need looking after. Fran, my room-mate, is happy to fulfil that role.

One morning, I discover what look like burn marks around my waist. Must be this new skirt rubbing, I think. Two days later and the mysterious blebs have spread. It's no use delaying: a visit to Matron must be made.

"Shingles!" she announces, far too cheerfully for my liking. "Nothing to be done except dab on calamine lotion."

Nothing to be done? I could scream in frustration. To a young girl, still a teenager and having suffered nothing more than an annual sore throat, this latest affliction proves to be torture. It feels like perpetual pins and needles. I can bear no clothes near the offending part of my body, and I can neither sit nor stand comfortably. And what makes matters worse, various girls have started to tell me horror stories.

'When the marks join up in a circle around your body, that's it! You've had it!'

Matron assures me that youth is on my side and it shouldn't hang around for too long.

Then I find there is no sleep to be had. Having to pace the floor all night is a new experience I do not wish to repeat. So once again, I'm back to Matron, who this time prescribes a sleeping tablet. A sleeping tablet? Will I collapse before I get into bed? Will I never wake? Naively I have no idea of the effects it may have upon me once it passes down my throat. Now Fran proves to be a friend indeed. My bedtime ritual of teeth, hair-brushing, diary, alarm clock, I dare not begin, in case the aforementioned tablet should knock me out before my head hits the pillow.

"Now don't worry, do your teeth and hair before you get into bed," soothes Fran. "You can write your diary and wind up your clock while I get a glass of water, and then you can take it."

I am a good patient and follow her orders. I believe that once this offending tablet has been swallowed, I will magically collapse into deep slumber. But no. Instead, I find that surprisingly, at first, nothing happens. But as I lie down and close my eyes, it's as if something is dragging me further and further downwards. When I try my hardest to count sheep, they float away from me until suddenly, I disappear. Almost the next moment, it seems, I open my eyes again to see Fran flinging back the curtains to let the morning sunlight stream in.

What happened to the night in between? Taking one little sleeping tablet has been an education.

Luckily for me, Matron is proved right and the shingles only last a week. My mother sounds quite put out when I ring her to tell her all about it and I have to explain in careful words that I hadn't wanted to worry her, but waited until it was all better.

Perhaps it is dawning on her that her little girl doesn't need her quite as much. Or that friends are taking her place. But with the free spirit of youth, I had no idea that she would want to know about my suffering. I thought I was doing her a favour.

Penny, next door to us at the end of the corridor, is another strong character: independent, not caring what anyone thinks of her, always wearing jeans and sandshoes, or 'pumps' as the Yorkshire folk call them. Her red dressing gown-cum-coat from last year has been discarded in favour of a moth-eaten fur coat, picked up from some jumble sale back at home in Leeds, which she is insisting upon wearing into the summer term. The jacket she acquired at Christmas, decorated with the head, paws and tail of a fox, has not made another appearance since, thankfully.

To add to her humble record collection, during the Easter vacation, she has added Jerry Lewis's 'Great Balls of Fire', which she frequently plays at top volume, that is, the highest her little turntable can produce. It makes a change from Glenn Miller.

There is always an endless stream of boyfriends and besides her home-grown admirers, like Ken and Dave who she picks up and drops as the whim takes her, she has also been out with practically every male student in our year deemed worthwhile. That makes at least a dozen out of the twenty-five we have of the species. Our year is College's introduction to the opposite sex. Being in the minority, they are naturally enjoying every advantage.

Other than my one dalliance last October, no other so-called boyfriend has come my way. I suffer some teasing from Penny, but I insist that Mr Right will one day show up. My description of the perfect partner, especially the bit about wearing 'a slightly worn corduroy jacket with leather patches at the elbows,' receives lots of chortling and ribbing from the others.

"No such person exists, my little Amelia," Penny says.

"One day," I retort, "one day, Cinderella shall go to the ball."

But, true to form, it is not I but Penny who can line up a male partner at the click of her fingers. Today, a wet Sunday afternoon in May, she parades up and down the corridor wearing the ankle-length dress she bought in Leeds at the weekend especially for the College Summer

Ball to be held in a few weeks' time. We all make suitable remarks of admiration, but I can't help feeling a tiny bit envious. Close fitting, low cut and sleeveless, it shows off her skinny-rib figure: not an ounce of fat anywhere to be seen.

Leaving Mary fussing around on the floor turning up the hem of the silky blue dress, I shut our room door and try to get back to revising. It's my second time around for the dreaded Homer's *Odyssey*.

"The exams are next month," I remind Fran, who isn't going to the Summer Ball either. She insists she is keeping faith with the Italian boyfriend she met on holiday.

Just as I settle on the bed with my open book, Fran jumps up.

"I've just thought of something. I haven't written to Leo." Anything to distract her from doing any actual work.

I give up the *Odyssey* as a lost cause. "Go on then. Tell me all about this Italian hunk of yours. When did you actually last set eyes upon him?"

At the mere mention of him Fran always turns coy, despite her usual blustering, casual nature about most things. Leo is definitely a sensitive subject.

"Well, as you are asking, I actually last set eyes upon him in Italy last summer: August the twenty-fifth, to be precise." She blushes. It is rare for anything to faze her and she has never been precise about anything. Obviously, the date was burned into her mind.

If Fran was still in Italy at the end of August, then she hadn't left herself much time to prepare for College. It had taken me almost the whole of the summer. But I keep my thoughts to myself. Instead I say, "How long were you in Italy?"

"Seven weeks and two days. I was at my grandmother's house most of the time."

"You've never told me where your dad was born. Was it here or in Italy?"

"Oh, in this country," Fran replies airily. She never boasts about her Italian family. Quite the opposite. In all the nine months I have known her, she rarely talks about them.

"Go on," I urge her. "I'd love to know a bit more."

Fran settles herself on her bed opposite mine and crosses her legs.

"Well, my grandparents came over to England to open a business after the First World War. Then Dad was born. A few years later, my grandfather decided to expand the business back in Italy and went back to manage it there."

"So why didn't your dad go as well?"

Fran fiddles with her long strands of shiny brown hair.

"He was at secondary school by then and so I gather, more English than Italian. He was sent to boarding school and met Mum there. They became teenage sweethearts. So romantic."

I gaze at her with envy.

"And you've been going to Italy to stay with your

grandparents every summer holiday?"

"Ever since I can remember."

"Then one summer, you had your own romantic moment when you met Leo."

She looks dreamy and wistful for a moment. Then she swiftly changes the subject.

"Do you know, I've never been anywhere in this country? Unless you count Cornwall, once, Youth Hostelling with school. Oh, and I've been to Wales for a Bank Holiday weekend."

I knew Fran hadn't been as far north as Yorkshire before, but this is the first time she has spelled out her limited travels, apart from Italy of course.

"So, what about the Cotswolds or the Lake District?"

"Nope. I've told you, I'd never seen a dry stone wall till I came here. Didn't know what one was!"

"I know. And I thought you were joking!"

Then I clap a hand to my forehead.

"Look, girl. To begin your education, you'd better come up home with me one weekend and I'll take you to Durham and show you the most magnificent cathedral in this country, in Europe even." I am starting to get excited. "You can see for yourself where I grew up on the coast, right next to the North Sea. It can get really windy and the waves lash over the pier sometimes. There's even a huge pit almost at the cliff edge, with its wheel constantly turning."

"What's a pit wheel, for goodness sake?"

I sigh. "Poor little ignorant Fran. Come and stay with me first. I'll show you the sights."

We sit in quiet reverie for a few seconds, contemplating the long summer holidays. My thoughts revolve around walking along the beach at home. The next few seconds prove that Fran's mind is firmly back in Italy.

"Look at the time," she squeals. "I'd better get on with my letter to Leo, if I want to catch the post."

And as she scrabbles around in the drawers at her desk looking for writing paper, I realise that she hasn't actually revealed anything much about that Italian boyfriend of hers. I wonder if she might be deliberately holding something back.

~~~

CHAPTER SIXTEEN

GOING FISHING

Gradually our excursions to the village of Moreton are beginning to make sense. So far, we have visited the school, the church and a farm, tramped around the surrounding fields and assessed the local shops. No one has actually spelled it out, but it is dawning upon us that the young children we will be educating should not be regarded as just little bodies sitting at a desk, struggling to read and write. Sometimes, children learn more by getting out of the classroom to find out about the world around them.

Just like today.

It's starting as a normal Monday morning. Our timetables have 'Education' written on them, from nine o'clock right through until lunch time. We are armed as usual with files, pens and notepaper, expecting more theory, more note-taking.

To our utter surprise, Miss Flowerdew announces, "Ladies! Our topic for today is, 'The River', our own environment. Just as you would take your class of juniors down to the river to collect specimens, so you are going to do the same."

Alison and I look at each other. We raise enquiring eyebrows as our lecturer continues, "Take jars, margarine tubs, yoghurt cartons, all the containers you can find. Get yourselves into groups and once you're down at the river, collect anything you can find beside and in the water. Today's the perfect sort of weather for it."

"Then what do we do with them?" Alison mutters.

As if she had heard, Miss Flowerdew is ready with the answer. "Then back in the lecture room, we will label them and see what we can find out about our specimens. They could be little fish, weed, river water, flowers, anything which attracts your attention."

We agree with each other that this sounds like fun, not work.

She went on, "If you need nets, there are a few in the stock cupboard down in the biology lab."

Clearly, she expects us to organise this ourselves, without her supervision. After all, once we are in schools, we will have at least thirty children to sort out. We should be quite capable of managing this outing on our own. The question of how our Education lecturer is going to spend the time does not enter our heads. Without any thought of the theory behind this venture, of the responsibility we ought to feel, I confess we simply regard this as licence to scurry off for a few hours.

So what if there are real things to be done, notes to write, follow-up work to complete? The sun is shining, the morning ahead of us. To the river we go.

Half an hour later, in groups of about six, nets in hand, jam jars and tubs in carrier bags, we stride through the streets with not a care in the world to go fishing. At the other end of town, we pass through a little gate in a stone wall and follow the footpath which leads to grassy fields and trees sloping down to the river. The greenery is bathed in May sunshine and the air filled with birdsong, and we are intoxicated with fresh air.

Perhaps that is why Alison and I go a little crazy. Or I should say, a little crazier than usual. As soon as we reach an open field, we turn into a double version of Maria from 'The Sound of Music', much to the amusement of the rest of our group. Although we're not technically on the side of a mountain, we have no reservations about singing '*The hills are alive*' at the tops of our voices. We feel very much alive today.

As I never tire of telling anyone who will listen, I have watched this film on widescreen, no less. In 1965 you were no one if you had not witnessed this musical. It was a special bus trip with Mam and Judith to the big, bright city of Newcastle, which we only ever visited once a year to buy new winter coats. We were all mesmerised by the dizzying scenes of mountain tops and the songs which stay in your head for ever more. There was even an interval as there is in the theatre. As Maria closed the huge door of Captain von Trapp's mansion to return to the nunnery, red curtains swept across in front of the screen and we all went to join the queue for two-and-sixpenny ice creams. We have no such luxury today, but we try to do justice to our opening song as we sing with joyful abandonment, conducting with fishing nets and swinging the bags of jars to the rhythm.

Our voices become overtaken by the sound of rushing water and the edge of the field eventually ends at the bank, where we find the river is shallow, rippling along over rocks and pebbles. With the sun warm on our backs, it seems to be the most natural thing in the world to fling off our flip flops and wade into the icy water. One or two of the group declare it is far too freezing, after delicately trying only a toe and decide to concentrate on any floral specimens among the grass. During the splashing and general larking about, Alison and I, of course, not only get our feet wet but also the edges of our jeans, although they are rolled up to just below our knees. We are revelling in the fact that there is no set timetable, no required questions to answer, only some vague instruction to collect what we fancy: we are set free.

It has been a few years since I plunged my bare white feet into clear, cold water. I am used to paddling in the sea, but this is quite different. The sea is moving, rushing, swirling. You hardly notice its numbing coldness until you are out and half way up the beach. A river is only moving in one direction, forever bringing down icy water from the hill streams. It freezes your toes the second you dip into its chilling depths.

"Nobody has thought to bring a towel," I grumble.

"You mean *you* forgot," Alison corrects me.

"Well, it wasn't just up to me. All we were told were containers."

"We're going to be teachers," she points out, "responsible for ourselves and little children, not robots in the army, simply doing as we're told."

"You are so right." I look at her. "Then why haven't you brought one?"

Although the sun hasn't altered the chill of the river, it has warmed the grass. Flip flops in one hand and jars full of squirming creatures in the other, we set off back to College and Miss Flowerdew, some of us still in bare feet until we reach the hard, cold pavements.

How we manage to get these slopping jars back to the biology lab, intact with river life, I do not know. We pour our specimens into tanks and set about investigating their names and life cycles. We draw pictures of the flowers and leaves and then press them under thick tomes of encyclopaedia.

It is so easy to write an account of our outing, because all the experiences are fresh in our minds: we have sung songs, felt the warmth of the sun on our faces and the cold water round our ankles. There is enough here to keep a class of children busy for a whole week with stories, poems, science, even music.

The more mature might argue that it is a totally unrealistic view of what teaching will be like once we are in charge of thirty children. Yes, perhaps we should have begun with questions to answer. But this is the child-centred way: you take your topic from what a child is interested in. Today, we have been like children. They are naturally curious and want to learn. This is the theory. Going out exploring comes first. The questions, answers and learning will happen next. It is a great ideal.

As we wend our way back to Dale House from the Lecture Block, following the path that snakes across the lawns, I reflect that what started out as a morning of freedom turned into an experience I can never forget. I learned a lot, not just for myself, but for the children I will teach in the future. College is showing me that education can be fun. No. More than that. Education *should* be fun.

Like today, when we went fishing.

CHAPTER SEVENTEEN

~~~

NIGHTS IN WHITE SATIN, PART ONE

Every dance I go to, I prepare myself for this being the one, the one where I will meet my mythical Mr Right. I haven't quite got the picture fully formed yet. I've only got as far as a picture in my head of him, wearing the shabby jacket with the elbow patches. Ideally, he would be playing the piano, which I concede is never going to happen, but I'm hoping it turns out it's one of his hobbies. The certain negatives are that he won't be wearing traditional student garb, that is, long scraggy hair, clinging T-shirt and flared jeans, ripped, frayed and patched. On the other hand, I'm not expecting pinstripes and shiny shoes. How I am going to recognise him across a crowded dance floor I have no idea.

Apart from the looks, the way people talk matters to me. Some men just aren't interested in where you come from or whether you like vinegar on your fish and chips. I have a clear idea of someone who is chatty and friendly, so that I don't feel I have to rack my brains for the next highly interesting comment. Fran says I'm looking for someone from over the rainbow.

Well, this next dance is no exception. I shall be on the look-out for a man who measures up to my particular criteria. It may not even be possible to hear anyone speak, to find out if they are friendly or not.

On Saturday, the latest highlight of the week is to be held at Leeds University featuring The Moody Blues, no less. It's been all the talk for days that the Uni has actually managed to book such a popular band. Despite continual complaints that the dances are seen as 'cattle markets' where all the men line the walls of the hall to 'eye up' what latest attractions have been bussed in for them, it seems that everyone who is anyone is going, cattle market or not. There are a few seats left on the hired coach and I don't want to miss out.

The Moody Blues are the next big thing in the pop world and I have at least heard the strains of 'Nights in White Satin' on Mary's transistor. In my innocence, having never seen the words written down, I imagine they are singing about *knights* dressed in white satin suits, which I think would not look amiss on Top of the Pops. But I am instructed by Penny, the fount of all knowledge in these matters, that the Moody Blues are warbling about nights spent in bed with satin sheets. I've never heard of such things. At home in the winter, we have flannelette ones to keep us warm. Penny says I have no idea about anything. I think she's right.

I actually prefer Simon and Garfunkel and their 'Bridge over Troubled Water', but the chances of them making an appearance up here in the north of England are non-existent.

As I said earlier, everyone is going to this dance, including the population of our corridor and possibly the whole of Dale House. All, that is, except Jill. She is an exception to several rules: having her old cloth bunnies in bed instead of a hot water bottle for instance and not understanding about satin sheets, about which I am glad I am not alone. Once she has made up her mind, nothing and no one can persuade her.

"I'm staying here and having a lovely, quiet night in," she insists. "Anyway, I'm in the middle of *Lord of the Rings*."

"Oh, good," says Penny. "While we're out, you can nick some blankets from the third years upstairs and make beds for our guests."

"What guests?" Jill asks in a high-pitched squeak.

"Ken and Dave, of course." Penny answers in her usual laid-back, nonchalant way. "Ken, you know, my old boyfriend from the sixth form. He's going to bring his friend for Mary. It's a trial run for the Ball."

They are all lounging around in Fran's and my room. Penny sits cross-legged on my bed crocheting, one of her more lady-like pursuits. Mary, with the loan of my sewing box, takes up most of the floor space stitching the hem of her ball gown, which she's been doing at every available minute. Meanwhile Fran has decamped to the library, declaring it impossible to concentrate on a last-minute essay. We have shooed her away, telling her, not unkindly, she'll get far more done than in the melee here.

I'm thinking that perhaps she's made the right choice. I get to the bottom of a page in *Mansfield Park* and realise I haven't taken in one word. The first time around, I only skip read it for our Jane Austen tutorials. Not as enjoyable as *Pride and Prejudice* had been my first impression. It looks as if I'll get no work done either. I put my bookmark in place to come back to it later.

"So, have you any idea where Ken and Dave are going to sleep?" I ask, although I can make a good guess at the answer. When Penny replies that they will be staying in the room she shares with Mary, I still show a reasonably fair imitation of a shock/horror expression, worthy of Elizabeth Bennet herself.

"On the floor," she adds indignantly, jabbing a finger downwards, resulting in a dropped stitch.

She puts her crocheting to one side, leans forward and rests her elbows on her knees in her usual ungainly fashion.

"Let's get down to brass tacks, as they say in Leeds,"

she says in a heavy Yorkshire accent. "The third years happened to mention, all four of them, that they're going home on Friday night for the weekend. Don't worry Jill, I didn't expect you to do this on your own. My plan is we'll all sneak up there and pinch – er, borrow – their blankets for Ken and Dave." Looking at the expression on Jill's face, Penny adds, "We'll put everything back on Sunday." She finishes triumphantly, "Then no one will be the wiser."

"And who is we?" I ask, thinking that this is not a situation ever encountered by the Bennet sisters. I can't imagine men being sneaked into Longbourn House or Jane Austen devising such a plan. In fact we have not moved much further into modern society ourselves. No men are allowed in rooms here at St Mag's after ten thirty.

Penny ignores my question and carries on with enthusiasm.

"When the dance finishes, we, that is Mary and me, come back in the college bus and the men come back in Ken's Mini. Now, they'll no doubt get back here first, so Jill…" Here she looks brightly and encouragingly at her. "This is where you come in. You nip down and let them in through the cellar door. No one sees them, they're nowhere near old Robbie's room, we enter legitimately through the front door and hey presto, they're in!"

Jill looks ready to explode. "So I've got to sit up twiddling my thumbs till one in the morning, just to open the flaming cellar door?"

"You could go to bed at ten and put your alarm on," Mary says, with a pin sticking out of the corner of her mouth, trying to be helpful.

"I don't want to go to bed at ten," retorts Jill.

Penny tries to calm the situation. "Listen, listen. It won't be one in the morning. We've got late night passes till twelve. That's not so bad, Jill, is it?"

Pleading looks win the day. Jill shrugs, not wanting to completely spoil things.

"Well, I suppose if they've got nowhere else to go..."

Penny and Mary look suitably relieved.

"That's my girl!" They both slap her on the back. "So, Friday night, girls, before we set off for the dance, it's blanket raiding time, OK?"

~~~

CHAPTER EIGHTEEN

NIGHTS IN WHITE SATIN, PART TWO

Lights are flashing, the beat is throbbing and people, mostly girls, are dancing wildly.

"When are they going to come on?" Fran has to put her mouth right up to my ear. In fact I don't catch every word of her sentence, but my brain can fill in the words that are lost. I shake my head and turn the palms of my hands upwards in a negative reply. Communication with this head-banging noise can only be done through sign language.

As usual, all the male university students line the perimeter of the hall. I don't fancy the look of any of them. Not a single corduroy jacket with patched elbows in sight. Sensibly, I keep that thought to myself.

Fran digs me in the ribs and points to the exit, making strangling motions with her tongue hanging out at the same time. Not being much of a fan of the warm-up group with some ridiculous name which is belting out songs before the headline Moody Blues, I'm happy to follow her through the writhing crowd. Out of the exit door, and at once the blast of cooler air, the feeling of more space and the relative quietness hits us.

"Thank goodness for that," I breathe.

"I could murder a glass of coke," gasps Fran. "Where's the bar?"

Before we can work out which way to go, a body comes hurtling towards us. Unfortunately it's not a potential dance partner who has been admiring us from afar, desperate to meet us, but Margaret from Dale House. She lives at the opposite end to us, in one of the big rooms with bay windows overlooking College Road. It takes her a few seconds to recover her breath.

"I've been looking all over for you lot," she says in a thick Geordie accent. I concentrate hard. I've only met her once or twice, but although from the North East myself, each time I hear her speaking, it's a strain to understand her Newcastle lilt, spoken at high speed. However, if I can't understand her, Fran has no hope at all.

Margaret continues in a gabble, "A girl has just passed a message on that there's been a phone call from St Mag's for anyone from the end corridor of Dale House and they should ring back straight away. You're the first I've come across. I haven't seen Penny or Mary anywhere."

I look at Fran. I think she's got the gist. Could it have been Jill ringing up? What's the emergency? Something at home?

We mutter our thanks to Margaret and dash off to find the nearest phone. A student who looks as if she belongs here tells us there's one on the wall in the entrance. Fran rummages in her bag for pennies. Between us, we manage to scrape together sixpence.

I lift up the receiver and then freeze. In a panic, I start to look round vaguely. "What on earth is the number? There's no directory here."

Fran pushes me to one side. "Here, give it to me. I know it off by heart. I'm always reversing the charges when I phone home."

I think that means she has to state the number she is ringing from each time. She grabs the receiver off me and dials without hesitation.

"If it was Jill who left the message, with a bit of luck, she might be there waiting in the common room for us to call back," I hiss at her over her shoulder.

It could be ages before anyone bothers to pick up the phone. And with most people here at the dance, Dale House will be near empty. Mercifully, someone at the other end answers, the bleeps go and Fran pushes the pennies in, one by one.

"Hello? This is Fran speaking… Oh Jill, we hoped it would be you. What's up?"

We look at each other nervously. Has someone died or been in a car accident? In my mind's eye, I'm already packing a bag and getting on the next express bus up to Durham.

Fran's face falls as she hears the reply. My stomach lurches.

"She found out? How, for goodness sake?"

I jump up and down with impatience to know what's going on.

"Who has found out what?"

Fran shushes me with a furious wave of her hand and continues her conversation with Jill. "Well, what d'you think we should do? I don't know where they are. We've never seen them all night… Don't worry, Jill, we'll do our best. Thanks for letting us know, anyway. See you later. Bye."

Fran puts the receiver down slowly. She has a serious look on her face.

"No one's died, thank the Lord."

I breathe a sigh of relief.

"But the bad news is, old Robinson's on the warpath. She's been snooping round and seen the made-up beds on the floor in Penny and Mary's room."

"But we made sure all our doors were shut before we left."

"I know we did. But apparently she wanted to have a

word with Mary about one of her essays she'd marked. So she went looking for her."

"We should have locks and our own keys," I say grimly. "Specially now we can vote in this month's General Election. Technically, College isn't *in loco parentis* now."

Fran interrupts me. "Look, we haven't got time to discuss all that. Yes, we know it's coming and it'll make life a whole lot easier. You're right, St Mag's is stuck in a time warp, making us sign out and all that palaver."

"You can say that again."

"But hey, right now, we've got a problem. When old Robbie knocked on her door, Jill says she just played the innocent about the whole matter and told her she had no idea why the blankets were there."

"No doubt she'll assume the obvious, that Pen and Mary have got blokes coming in tonight."

"They'll be out on their ear, if that does happen," Fran says in a serious tone.

I nod in agreement. "Remember when that girl along Abbey corridor in main College was seen letting a bloke through her window at midnight? She was sent packing on the next train home."

"Well, let's not even think about that," says Fran briskly. "We'd better go hunting for Penny and Mary."

"So where are Ken and Dave going to sleep tonight?" I ask, just before we open the door to the dance hall and enter through the wall of sound.

"That's their problem," she mutters. "First things

first, we've got to make sure they don't set foot inside Dale House."

Laughing and shushing in turn, four of us stumble up the cellar stairs in the dark.

"Shut up! Jill's probably asleep," Penny says in a stage whisper that echoes up to the high ceilings. "She wasn't best pleased when I phoned her to ask if she would put all those blankets back."

"I bet she's awake. And on the last page of *Lord of the Rings*," I giggle, high on three glasses of fizzy Coca Cola and dancing to The Moody Blues.

But the corridor is silent and no light peeps from under Jill's door. Penny and Mary take off their shoes and tiptoe along the smooth, cold lino to their room at the end of the corridor, hissing some fairly loud goodnights. Fran collapses onto her bed, exhausted after the excitement of the evening, and instantly falls asleep in her clothes.

I crawl between the sheets, lie back on the pillow and try to rid my dulled ears of the constant, thumping drum beat. With closed eyes, I can still see flashing lights behind my eyelids. What would real satin sheets feel like, I wonder? Would they soothe my aching feet?

Sleep does not come immediately.

There goes yet another dance with no sign of a Mr Anybody, never mind Mr Right. There's always next Saturday. And two more years after that. As for tonight being a trial run for the Summer Ball, Penny would have to come up with another plan for Ken and Dave.

I pull my tartan rug up to my chin, feeling that I will never take a comfortable warm bed for granted and try to imagine just what it must be like sleeping cold and crushed up in a Mini.

CHAPTER NINETEEN

~~

ANYONE FOR TENNIS?

I yell down the corridor, "Anyone for tennis?"

"Wait for me. I'm in your group, remember?" answers Penny. She emerges from her room dressed, as I am, in our regulation PE uniform. It consists of a yellow Aertex T-shirt and wrap-around brown skirt made from a thick serge material. Catwalk model potential I think not.

She adjusts the tops of her white ankle socks. "Not exactly tennis gear," she grumbles. "Let's put it this way, we'd never be allowed to set foot in Wimbledon. But it'll have to do."

"And that's not the only reason we wouldn't be allowed on that hallowed ground, because I don't know about you, but I can't play!"

Then Penny lets out a piercing shriek. "Where did you dig up that ancient racket?"

I hold up the offending article and twang each plastic string. The wooden frame is scratched and worn. It feels heavy and cumbersome as I attempt to do a practice serve.

Penny ducks out of the way. "Watch it! You're dangerous with that thing."

"This is an antique," I say, pretending to be offended. "Well, as good as."

"Whose was it? Your great-grandmother's?"

"Not exactly. My sister bought it at Woolworth's for two and six when she was eleven."

Jill comes out of her room, leans on the doorframe and gazes with undisguised amusement at the spectacle of me in my fetching PE kit, waving my racket around.

"You want to send that thing to a museum."

"Not you as well. It's the only one I possess. Couldn't afford to buy another. Not like moneybags here."

I nod to Penny, who is now brandishing her own weapon, sleek, shiny and brand new.

"Here, borrow mine," says Jill. "My group's not having PE today."

I fling my old racket through the open door of my room. "Thanks. I'm really looking forward to learning how to play properly. I do know how to score, but how do you really serve? You know, like Rod Laver."

"Did you not do tennis at school?" asked Penny.

I shake my head. "Sadly, in my whole school career we only ever played once. That was when we had a student and about thirty of us had to share four courts. It was useless."

"Come on, stop dancing around," Penny replies. "Let's get a move on. We'll be late."

I assure Jill that I will take great care of her racket, which isn't exactly new, but as it's in far better condition than mine, it had obviously cost slightly more than half a crown. Giving her a thumbs-up sign, I make a hasty exit to catch up with Penny, who is already halfway down the stairs.

About two hours later, we crawl back up the stairs to our corridor on the first floor, hot, sweaty and breathless.

"Coffee, coffee! Put the kettle on, Jill," Penny shouts.

Jill pokes her head out of her room. "When are you trying for Wimbledon, then?"

I groan and sit grumpily on Jill's bed. "Thanks for the loan of the racket, but there was no help from old Watson."

"Why? What happened?"

"Well, she said, in her usual bright tone, 'You must all know how to play tennis. So off you go, get into fours and find a court.'"

"And?" Jill stands with the kettle, waiting to go and fill it up.

"And nothing. That was it. I'm no further forward." I lie back on the bed to stretch my weary legs. "I still don't know how to play. I'll have to resign myself to simply watching tennis every summer for the rest of my life."

Jill disappears with the kettle as I make strangulating gestures at my throat.

Penny comes in with three mugs in readiness for our much-needed drink. "Yes, it was one of those 'going off' lectures, wasn't it? Where we did everything and the lecturer did *nowt*." She emphasises the last word in her usual Yorkshire way.

"But, Amelia, did you manage at least to serve?" asks Jill, reappearing to plug in the kettle.

I put on my most miserable face.

"I couldn't even get the ball across the net into the opposite side! I just don't have the strength in my arm!"

"Well, it saves you the bother of buying a new tennis racket. By the way girls, brace yourselves, I've got some bad news."

Penny passes her the mugs. "Oh no! Come on then. Tell us everything. We can take it."

"It's Mr McNulty again."

"I thought our friendly caretaker had been quiet for a while."

"No, you mean, *we've* been quiet," I say. "We've kept to our promise of tiptoeing at bedtime."

"It isn't the problem of noise this time," Jill says, passing round the hot mugs of coffee, flavoured as usual with powdered milk. "It's yogurt cartons."

"Yogurt cartons?" Penny and I speak in unison.

Jill grins. "Apparently, we're throwing yogurt cartons onto his garden."

We can't believe this latest complaint.

Jill explains. "You know when we've been keeping things cool on our outside window sills in this warm weather, like butter and … you get it, yogurts?" She starts to laugh. "I thought some of mine had been going missing lately. Well, they've been falling down into Mr McNulty's garden."

"And he thinks you're throwing them down deliberately as rubbish!"

Then all three of us are laughing.

Jill continues, "So the message from Robbie goes that two of us must go downstairs after tea tonight and apologise once again."

Writing my diary in bed tonight, I contemplate how I haven't learned to play tennis or how to serve aces like Rod Laver. However, I have discovered that I was never going to be a star on the Wimbledon courts. As well as knowing how to accept my limits, I have also learned how to make a humble apology, even though it seems totally unjustified.

As Jill and I grumbled to each other while we rinsed our coffee mugs in the bathroom sink earlier this evening, we miraculously came up with the perfect solution: all it would take, would be for College to provide us with a fridge.

CHAPTER TWENTY

~~~

DECISIONS

It's decision time. Time to decide where we are all going to live, move and have our beings. It has to be either in digs for the second year and back into Halls of Residence for the third year, or vice versa.

The general rule is that second years are 'out' and third years 'in'. There is even a second-year common room aptly named 'non-res'. Some students choose one of the few college flats dotted around town, widely regarded as havens of peace where you actually own a front door key and a college cleaner keeps the place reasonable. Some students stay there for the remaining two years.

Neither Jill nor I fancy the idea of a flat. We love being part of this establishment, having the feeling we almost own the place. Isn't that the whole point of being here? In a flat we'd be too far away, divorced from the vitality of college life, away from the green lawns and the trees and the smell of polished floors in the corridors. So we decide to keep to the normal procedure, which, in our opinion, is by far the best option: digs for second year, back in for third, when you can more or less choose which Hall to live in. Our companions on the corridor, however, choose the opposite. It's a college flat for Fran, Jill's room-mate Pat, along with Mary and Penny. And a sad farewell to all the vintage 78 records.

We all feel free to go our own way. But I wonder if anyone has stopped to ponder that our communal way of life will cease for ever. I believe firmly however, that something different will evolve to take its place. The only point I am unsure about is that I have become used to our good laughs, our long conversations and even the enforced tiptoeing every night to our single bathroom. I can do without that last point, but I imagine Jill and me finding digs on our own too quiet and lonely.

I decide to have a word with Alison, my friend from Cottages, who works with me almost every day both in my Education group and also main English, so already I know we get on. Jill, carefree as ever, raises no objection to my broaching the subject with her about sharing digs.

On the day of our next instalment of the ongoing project around the village of Moreton, Alison and I find ourselves standing side by side at the edge of a field. Tentatively I broach the subject of where to live next year. I feel uneasy. What if she says no? What if she wants to say no, but doesn't know how to say it? I shift my feet, clad in walking shoes, to a slightly less wet patch of mud.

Happily, her reply is positive. "Amelia, I am so pleased and relieved you have asked."

I still offer her a get-out clause. "Well you can think about it and let me know later on."

Ten minutes later and we are both holding our noses. "Cor, this farmyard does pong," I whisper. We aren't taking much notice of what the lovely Miss Flowerdew is talking about. She is holding forth at the front while we skulk at the back.

"Have you got any notes about that farm machinery?" Alison whispers.

Our Moreton project is slowly wearing us down and most of us have lost all enthusiasm.

I show her my notepad. "I've just done a few sketches."

"What a great idea."

Using the top of a stone wall as an uneven desk, she begins making quick pencil strokes. Miss Flowerdew's voice drones on in the background.

"Well, what do you think?" I hiss. It has only been a few minutes since I asked the all-important question, but I can't wait any longer.

Alison doesn't even look up from her drawing. "What about?"

"Digs, you dumb cluck!"

"That's my phrase, and anyway it only sounds right in a Yorkshire accent." Her pencil is poised now. "Seriously,

I've been wondering what to do myself. My own room-mate mentioned something about joining up with a girl I don't know very well, and I don't fancy living with them in a three. If I go with you and Jill, we'll still need one more."

By now, the rest of the group have moved on to look at the battery hens. With the squawking from both poultry and students in the background, we agree to find a fourth party to join us. I remind her that the list on the first-year notice board has to be filled in by the end of next week, but Alison has an idea already. She tells me she knows someone in the first year who might be interested: a school friend from back home. She's called Brenda, does main History and so will know Jill. I agree – that sounds like a plan.

Alison folds up her notes and sticks her pencil in the back pocket of her jeans. One of our group is waving and pointing.

"Looks like we're going into the farmhouse for goodies. Come on!"

I feel a mixture of relief and elation. It's decided. These days, when time plays out steadily, only one year ahead is the future. Our future is a year in digs.

CHAPTER TWENTY-ONE

~~~

SEPTEMBER 1970

COLD BUT CLEAN

"Is Fran coming back to College?" Alison, in a flustered state, runs down the stairs into the hallway, where I am standing surrounded by a year's worth of luggage. Pete shuts the inner glass door behind us and my mother eyes the cornices for cobwebs.

"What are you talking about? Of course, she is. I've just stayed with her for a week during the summer, and the last thing she said was, 'See you in September'."

This is how I am greeted into Number 3 Northgate, a three-storey red-brick terraced house, our home for the year. The directions read: 'Turn left at the junction opposite Cottages, down the bank and left again.' Just around the corner from College, really. We think ourselves very lucky.

Mrs Parker, our landlady, appears on the scene and Alison whispers to me that she'll fill in the details later when everyone is gone.

For weeks now, Mam has been mostly concerned about the cleanliness of our digs. On first appearances, Northgate does not disappoint on that score. Everything is spick and span down to the gleaming gnomes guarding a small pond in the long front garden.

I can tell that Mam is happy with the situation by the way she scrutinizes, with approval, Mrs P's brown overall of thick cotton serge. Ancient, but spotlessly clean, it looks as if it began its early service among the tables of an army canteen. As we follow her up the stairs, I notice that her straight, grey hair is held back at each side with a severe brown clip, as far as I can see, her only adornment. All the housewifely women in my life dress themselves with charm and care: my mother with her colourful beads to match her blouse; my aunty with her gold bracelets that jangle as she sets the table; my grandmother with her double stranded set of pearls and a twinkle in her eye. In contrast, my landlady seems to choose practicality above all else. Her straight hair clips match the straight line of her mouth.

My mother glides her white lace-edged handkerchief down the banisters, metaphorically speaking of course. When my Aunty Alice was in service in the 1920s her mistress did just that, finding not one speck of dust on the delicate square of pure white cotton, so my aunty passed the test. Had it been otherwise, I suppose she would have been sent packing, back to my grandmother's in disgrace. In my situation, I imagine Mam marching up to College and hammering on the door of our esteemed Principal, demanding different digs for her daughter.

Mrs Parker conducts a tour of the house, pleasantly enough, but I notice she is opening only those doors where we students are to be allowed entry.

"This is the room where you four girls will have your meals and work in the evening." She quietly ushers my mother and me past the front sitting room, along the passage and into a room which dimly overlooks the back yard through cream-coloured net curtains.

"There's a gas fire for extra heat in the winter and shelves for your books." She gestures towards the alcoves on either side of the chimney breast. Her voice is thick Yorkshire, but devoid of emotion, without any of the usual rise and fall.

"And if you could let me know if you want a bath, just open the hatch doors and I'll be in the kitchen."

I get the impression that Mrs P is expecting us to be model students, hunched over our books long into the dark evenings, humbly grateful for our solitary weekly bath.

Gazing round what is to be our refuge and haven for three terms, I notice covers everywhere: on the backs and seats of our easy chairs and across the sideboard, vacant of any vase or ornament. Even the fitted carpet is concealed by small mats variously arranged where we might place our feet. With a lonely clock standing on its own in the middle of the mantelpiece and shelves empty and waiting to be filled with our education manuals and essential novels, the room is lacking in both comfort and character.

My loving mother, happy and content that all seems well, at least in the practical sense, leaves for home with Pete. My brother-in-law has performed his usual strong-arm feat of hauling my cases up the flight of stairs and depositing them on the landing. I have yet to discover which room is to be my abode, as Mrs Parker has left us to decide among ourselves.

Much to Pete's relief, my trunk has been left at home, in favour of a couple of suitcases and an assortment of bags. Because we shall be looked after in a house, we have been informed that not so many possessions are needed. I try not to think about my coffee jar, languishing in Mam's pantry. Not to mention the precious yellow teapot, with its thin gold stripes and matching cups and saucers, loaned out when someone's parents come to visit. They are all redundant as there's no kettle as in Dale House, merrily steaming away on the lino floor, to make friendly late-night cuppas. We'll be totally reliant on what Mrs Parker provides for us.

After waving Mam and Pete off from the front gate and calling out lots of thank yous, I walk back up the long garden path. The front door is painted dark green with a gleaming brass handle in the middle. Above the bay window I notice two bedrooms and on the second floor, in the attic, another room: my all-time would-be favourite. Wouldn't that be a dream come true: a little haven up in the roof space? Lying in bed, listening at night to the rain and the wind on the tiles, waking up to the sun streaming in through the dormer window.

There I go again. My mother is right. I read too many stories.

I step into the house. All is quiet. There is a smell of polish and a faint whiff of meat roasting in the oven. It reminds me that lunch back at home was a very long time ago. Mrs Parker is nowhere to be seen. Probably retreated into her kitchen: obviously her own domain, as the back recesses of the house were not included on her tour. Maybe, she's producing a feast of a meal for us. So far, our landlady is proving to be a woman of few words. I'm guessing we won't find out what's on the menu until we open those hatch doors and see what comes through.

Alison is in our dining-cum-study room. I shut the door behind me. At least, here is privacy.

"Have Jill and I got the attic?" I ask, hopefully.

"No such luck. None of us have. You two are in the first bedroom at the top of the stairs, next to the bathroom, you jammy pair!"

My attic room would have to remain a dream. One day, some day, I shall have a house of my own, and it will have proper stairs leading up to rooms in the roof. My disappointment doesn't last long. Far too much to think about.

"Have you picked a room then?"

"Brenda and I are in the second one, where you turn left at the top of the stairs. She fancied it because it's the biggest. And we did arrive first."

I hold up my hands in complete compliance. Next door to the bathroom wins over the size of a bedroom.

We have become a foursome. Alison has teamed up with her old school friend Brenda, who in the summer term had found herself in need of a room-mate. How will this turn out, I wonder, after the communal life of last year's corridor?

But Alison's thoughts are elsewhere. The expression on her face changes. She frowns.

"So, do you really think Fran hasn't left College?"

I slump down in an easy chair, on top of all the covers.

"Can I bag this one? It's lovely and comfortable. It beats a hard chair at the study table or the bed like we had last year." I wriggle about a bit to emphasise the point. "Where've you got the idea that she's not coming back, for goodness sake?"

"As soon as I got here, I went up to College to look at the Teaching Practice list. And there was her name. Crossed off! She was going to be in the same school as me. Now I'll be all on my own."

I couldn't understand it. "But I just saw her, less than a month ago when I stayed at her house for a few days.

We went to London together on the train." I think for a few moments. "Then she was going to Italy for the last two or three weeks of August. She never mentioned leaving. Why would she leave, anyway?"

"God knows. She's your friend, you know her better than I do," groans Alison, claiming the armchair opposite mine.

"She probably hasn't done her Play essay. Although we both did a few observations while I was down there, so she must have meant to do it." I rack my brains for more clues. "Come to think of it, she was way behind in her work. She never finished her Home and School file and that was due in months ago. But there was no mention of even the possibility of her leaving."

"Or she didn't want to tell you," Alison points out.

"How about, when Jill arrives, we walk up to College and have another look at that list? Just to make sure. By the way, where is Brenda?"

"Upstairs, unpacking. That's what you should be doing. I'll give you a hand, if you like. We can sort the books out later."

"Which shelves do you want?"

Alison is anything but indecisive. "Brenda and I have bagged those in the left alcove and Jill and you can have the ones on the right."

I bend down to take a closer look at our gas fire, with its three columns of white blocks where the flames should be. It's the same as the one at home in the living room. Mam generally has that turned up to maximum to counteract the draught blowing through the gap under the door. I imagine cosy nights here in our little study room, all of us curled up in our easy chairs, engrossed in novels, reading out the best bits and wading through great thick history books.

"Let's try the fire on."

"Oh, I wouldn't bother with that." Alison sounds quite dismissive. "I've already had a go at putting it on. The knob's been altered so that we can only turn it to the first notch, so we're restricted to heating up the middle bar only."

I shrug. "Well, we'll have to pull our chairs up closer to the flames and hope there's no draught howling in under the door."

I'm beginning to think that Mrs Parker is going to prove to be the stingiest landlady of all. Clean maybe, but stingy.

CHAPTER TWENTY-TWO

~~~

'SMILE A LITTLE, SMILE A LITTLE, AS YOU GO ALONG'

A letter arrives this morning. Our first full day in Number 3, Northgate. It is true. Fran has left College. She writes that she is to marry Leo, her Italian beau.

I am bereft of words. Over the summer, we stayed in each other's homes. I introduced her to the unsurpassable Durham Cathedral. She showed me the relentless traffic in Trafalgar Square. I took a photograph of her there, standing tall and bulky in her red PVC Mary Quant-style coat, her long hair tangled in the wind, the famous fountain in the background. I vividly remember my friend waving me off at the railway station. She was full of excitement at the thought of going to Italy for a fortnight, before ... before coming back to College? Try as I might, I cannot recall if she actually said, 'See you in September'. I told Alison that, but perhaps I might have dreamed it.

Still, neither had she said she would never see me again. Even if her plans were already made, those words would have been too painful to hear.

As I hand the letter round for the others to read at the breakfast table, my gut feeling tells me I will never again see my 'Cockney' friend Fran.

There is more sad news to come. When we next meet some of our old corridor gang going across to lectures, they announce that Jill's old room-mate, Pat, is another one who has not returned. She always maintained she had no imagination. That you must have to be a successful teacher. From our original eight in Dale House, we have slumped to four.

Mary and Penny tell us they are living in a college house way down by the river, at least half an hour's walk away. Although we exchange hearty promises of getting together, it seems likely we may only see them at odd times. Jill and I, having 'disposed' of our respective first year room-mates, are brought closer together. We have common interests as well as differences. Every night we lie in our single beds quietly talking and talking after we have switched off the lights.

A framed rhyme hangs on our bedroom wall, a facile verse, certainly not great poetry. But it amuses us to recite it before sleep overtakes us.

Smile a little, smile a little,
As you go along.
Not alone when things are pleasant,
But when things go wrong.

I don't think either Jill or I will ever forget it.

We certainly have to keep smiling about the pies. Regular as clockwork, Mrs Parker serves them once a week for our evening meal. We have found she always keeps strictly to the rules laid down for the menu which college landladies must provide: soup and a main course one day, a main course and a dessert the next. Without fail. Never soup *and* a dessert. That would be breaking the rules.

During our first week, Brenda announces that she doesn't eat bread with soup. From that day on, we are only given three slices, never four. We imagine Mrs P with her ear to the hatch.

The routine goes thus: the hatch doors from our dining room to the kitchen open with no warning and out come our dinners. That is, straight out onto the floor if one of us is not in the vicinity to catch them, although we dare not try out this theory, lest there should be broken crockery and spilt vegetables or worse to clear up. We have heard neither a 'Had a good day, girls?', nor, 'Isn't the weather dreadful?' No pleasantries are ever offered.

Therefore, we offer none in return, and communication is reduced to an absolute minimum. There is an exception: the question as to whether any of us require a bath. A soak in the tub must be planned for and requested beforehand. 'Soak' may not be the right word, as the amount of hot water never rises more than two or three inches. We have resorted to a quick in and out.

This is no hardship, for at home our bathroom is not a place in which to linger. With no central heating, Mam often resorts to a standing oil heater which only slightly takes the chill off the freezing cold room. And then the back boiler behind our coal fire in the kitchen is not the most efficient. Our so-called hot water at home is little more than tepid. Often, I resort to covering myself with flannels as I lie in the big green bath with the brass taps. The cold one in the washbasin has never worked, so we are forced to clean our teeth over the bath. You could say I am used to being without any sort of luxury. At least, at home we do possess an indoor toilet. Some of my friends are still using ancient privies down the back yard, even in these modern times of 1970.

Back to Mrs Parker and her limited menu. If it's Tuesday, it must be pie night. The pies come through as if by robot, complete with mashed potato and peas already doled out on our individual plates. We close the hatch doors and wrinkle our noses in disgust. They are obviously shop-bought pies with thick, strong-smelling gravy poured over like a dark brown river running into a lake in the middle of the plate.

Famished as ever, we tuck in with enthusiasm, despite the dubious aroma. Jill is the first to plunge in with knife and fork. Revealed under the top crust is not chunky pieces of succulent steak but a pool of grease.

"Look at this," she squeals, and we try to shush her immediately. Mrs P has form when it comes to listening in. "Try yours, Amelia. See if it's the same."

I do and it is. Brenda's and Alison's show the same greasy oasis.

"I can't detect a scrap of meat," I say, peering at the soggy mess.

"Look at all the thick pastry round the edge," moans Alison. "It's as hard as rocks."

Still concerned about the possibility of an ear on the other side of the hatch, Jill whispers, "We can't possibly eat these. What the heck are we going to do with them?"

Sending all four pies back, uneaten, is unthinkable.

"How do we get out of it?" Alison looks half-scared, half delighted at our predicament. Then she has one of her usual, wonderful brainwaves. "We'll nip upstairs and tip the grease down the sink."

I forgot to whisper. "What! We can't do that. All four of us?"

Brenda stands up and starts gathering our pies onto one plate and scraping off as much gravy as she can. She is what I would describe as a big girl. Not overweight, just generally big. With her laid-back manner, I get the feeling she's the sort not to care very much about what anybody says or thinks.

"Give them to me," she sighs. "I'll take them all." And in a loud voice, "I'm just going up to the toilet."

Before she disappears out of the door, balancing the four pies on a plate, I hastily cover them with a serviette.

The three of us are in a state of nervous excitement, in case she meets our seldom-seen landlady, or even the more elusive Mr Parker, on the stairs. None of us have given any thought to how Brenda might explain why anyone would walk into the bathroom carrying four pies.

Five minutes later, our brave house-mate reappears. "There! That's the best I can do," she says in her Yorkshire, matter-of-fact way. She slaps the pies back onto our plates. By now, the mash and the peas are clear cold. The grease is drained out, but the remaining meat, what there is of it, is tough and gristly. Alison was right, the pastry proved to be hard as the hobs of hell itself. We chew through them as best we can, but I must admit, a good deal is sent back through the hatch.

Tonight, Jill and I recite our little verse with gusto. We have had reason to smile a little while things go wrong on several occasions since the beginning of term.

Two weeks on and communication at Northgate between us and she-who-shall-be-found-in-the-kitchen is next to nil. We reckon, though, that Mrs Parker must have got the message, as we have had no more pies for our evening meal, which pleases us greatly.

Privately, I suspect she saw the grease round the basin plughole.

CHAPTER TWENTY-THREE

~~~

A JOURNEY INTO
THE UNKNOWN

Teaching Practice has appeared on the horizon. Our experience last year at Moreton Village School was a mild affair, with three of us together in one room. This time it is to be the real thing: one student, one class, thirty children.

Alison and I are horrified to find we are allocated to schools in Teesside, to me an unknown no-man's land, not in Yorkshire and yet not quite belonging to my own north-eastern corner of the world. Doubtless the locals would disagree. I imagine it full of factories and ICI works, belching smoke and polluting the seaside air.

And then there is the added trauma of having to settle in to yet another set of digs during weekdays, just when we are getting used to Mrs P.

I have been working non-stop for days now. Teaching Practice means an endless number of lesson plans, resulting in having to sit up all night, chewing fingernails and ends of pencils and deciding on the difference between Aims and Objectives. Our little study room, even with the gas fire set to its allowed maximum, which is in fact its minimum, proves to be a cosy if not an overly-warm retreat.

Out of the four of us, Alison and I are going into schools first. Jill and Brenda, in their different Education groups, have to wait until the second half of the autumn term.

"I don't know whether I'm envious of you two, or relieved," I say one evening.

I am sitting at the dining table, which doubles as a study worktop. I've been rattling away at my typewriter since teatime, finishing off a particularly tricky scheme of work. The light outside the window, rapidly fading to a damp autumn gloom, reflects the mood indoors. Two of us grow more morose each day as the departure for Teesside looms closer.

"Relieved about what?" asks Brenda. She tries to push a number of newly acquired text books onto her already packed shelf in the alcove shared with Alison.

I was right about our pathetic gas fire. We are forced to draw our chairs to within a few feet of the fireplace to feel any benefit. Sitting at the table, the chilliest place in the room to work, I need my thickest woollen cardigan draped round my shoulders.

"Well," I explain, "One way to look at it is, I'm partly relieved that we're getting our Teaching Practice over and done with. But on the other hand, you two have the luxury of more time to prepare for the coming doom. Plus, you'll get to do Christmassy things."

Alison looks up with felt pen poised above a work card at the opposite end of the table. "I'd give anything not to have to get on that coach on Sunday afternoon."

My grumbling is not yet done. "At least you're out of the town in a nice little village school. I'm right in the middle of Thornberry." And with a dramatic air, I growl, "The heart of the industrialised North."

Alison is ready with her answer. "But I'm all on my own. You're lucky to have Penny in your school and in digs."

"Aw!" says Jill with mock sympathy. "Will you be all lonely?"

"It's all right for you," sniffs Alison. "But remember, I'll have no one to argue with during the evening."

"That's true." I smile. "There'll be nobody there to tell off for making a mess."

Alison is constantly pointing out to Jill and me that the shelves on our side of the fireplace are the polar opposite of her ultra-neat ones. With the added pressure of Brenda letting us all know, by her running commentary, that she is now arranging her books in alphabetical order, I promise faithfully that Jill and I will sort out our chaotic-looking piles. "I just haven't had the time," is my lame excuse.

Alison, back to her cheerful self, says, "We've only been here a couple of weeks and already I'm finding out all your worst points."

I look back at the sheet of paper in my typewriter. "My very worst point at this moment is that I've still got this Maths scheme to finish and I've just noticed another blooming typing error." And I reach for the little, white bottle of correcting fluid.

At last, everything is done. I've seen Mr Ramshaw about Music, Mr Taylor about RE, Miss Flowerdew about Environmental Studies, Miss Hindmarch about Reading and Writing and Miss Watson about everything. The latter is my Teaching Practice tutor, and she must check all my preparation.

I worry that the theory we have learned so far might not work out in practice in the classroom. Let's say I don't feel too confident.

Sunday is the dreaded day with a chilly, late September feel in the air. As we wait on the pavement for our cases to be stacked into the boot of the coach, I feel a small amount of comfort when I catch sight of Penny, who is to be my partner-in-crime both in digs and in school. I'm glad to have a familiar face from Dale House. She is already on board and saving a couple of seats for Alison and me.

We wave half-heartedly to Jill and Brenda, who have loyally walked up to College to see us off. My heart is in my mouth. Penny says that hers is pounding.

An hour later, Alison is one of the first to be dropped off. We gaze enviously out of the window at the village where she has been allocated. There's a picturesque backdrop of a hill with a definite conical peak. Someone tells us it's a famous local landmark, poetically named, Roseberry Topping. I say it sounds more like a dessert. No one feels like laughing. We promise each other we will climb it one day, in some happy, distant future. On this Sunday evening, as the sky becomes greyer and gloomier by the minute, our minds are preoccupied with what the next few weeks hold in store for us.

We leave the countryside behind and as the bus winds its way deep into Teesside's maze of urban streets, the light finally fades. After what seems an age since we set off, Penny and I are almost the last to reach our destination. Taking our cases wearily, we stand in the cold under a street lamp to peer at the slip of paper showing the address of our Teaching Practice digs: 25 Ashton Street.

Fortunately, the coach driver has deposited us right on the corner at number one, and we count the doors down the length of the terrace to find our new home. Penny lifts the heavy iron knocker and lets it fall, twice. The sharp noise resounds around the quiet, lonely-looking street, void of any people or passing cars.

Almost immediately, the door opens to reveal a smiling round-faced woman with a bright flowery pinny around her waist, not unlike the ones my mother usually wears. Apparently, our new landlady has been on tenterhooks, or so she says, waiting for us to arrive. She ushers us inside, at the same time calling for her husband to relieve us of our luggage.

Mr and Mrs Stewart are proving to be the perfect couple to receive a pair of apprehensive students on a chilly autumn evening. In the warm kitchen, we are given a supper of meat and potato pie, tasty and, unlike the debacle of Mrs Parker's greasy, shop-bought offerings, definitely home-made, with piles of mushy peas, as much as we can devour. After huge portions of Mrs Stewart's strawberry trifle, proudly named by Mr Stewart as being her speciality, we are shown to our room at the top of the narrow stairs, with twin beds and a wardrobe to share. Small, but warm and cosy. The parting shot before we unpack our cases is that there's plenty of hot water for baths and showers whenever we like.

The contrast with Northgate is remarkable.

CHAPTER TWENTY-FOUR

INTRODUCING
MISS HARDY

"I can't eat that, can you?" whispers Penny.

It's Monday morning early, really early. We each have a plate in front of us on the table in the dining room with the biggest fried breakfast I have ever encountered.

I answer in an equally low voice, "Well, maybe the bacon, but I couldn't possibly swallow the fried egg or that big fat sausage."

I push the offending items to one side. The smell emanating from a sizzling frying pan has been wafting up the stairs since we dragged ourselves from our beds at six o'clock.

Mrs Stewart bustles in with a heap of toast and a pot of marmalade. "Come on now girls. Eat up. It'll do you good to start with a proper breakfast. Set you up for the day. For your first day in school."

As if we need reminding.

"You're going to need lots of energy. Just ask for anything else you want."

Penny and I put on a brave smile and say thank you. How can we possibly tell her that a simple bowl of cornflakes would suit us better? It isn't that the bacon and eggs are badly cooked. Far from it. They are perfectly fried and smell delicious. Well, they would in any other circumstances, or on a different sort of day. A day when we are not going into school for the first time as trainee teachers. A day when we are not going to have to face a sea of thirty little faces. But at this minute we feel sick, sick in our stomachs at the very thought. I have already turned my insides out whilst brushing my teeth.

We do our best with Mrs Stewart's well-meaning offering and hurry off to gather up all our prepared paraphernalia and set off to face the day.

Once inside the school doors, we part company, Penny to her top infants, made up of children aged six and seven, and I make my way to the younger class, referred to as the 'middles'. They are one up from Reception, or 'the babies', as some of the older members of the profession insist on calling them. At least my class should, in their second year at school, have made a start with learning to read and might even be able to write a little.

In the classroom is that same smell I'd encountered at Moreton village school: unmistakably, a mixture of chalk dust, pencil shavings, Plasticine and something else which I'm not sure about. I stand nervously and silently beside Mrs Hudson, my class teacher, as she shows me the enormous register opened at her desk. There seems to be an endless list of names. Meanwhile, the children busy themselves fairly noisily.

"There are nineteen boys. Some of them are fairly well below average." She motions slightly with her head towards a little group who are supposed to be 'reading' in the reading corner. I notice their concentration on any one book lasts only a matter of seconds.

"That child there," Mrs Hudson continues in a voice meant only for my hearing, "is one of seven and very neglected. Attention seeking. We'll have to watch him."

I glance at her and see that she seems not in the slightest bit perturbed by the problem. I feel very perturbed.

"And this little boy," she goes on, indicating the nearest table. A pathetic-looking child, with a gaping hole at the shoulder of his scruffy jumper where the seam is coming apart, vainly tries to force a jigsaw piece into the wrong place. He gives up and tosses the triangle shape across the desk, then picks up a rectangle. I can see it's a pentagon he needs. I wonder if he knows that word. I wonder if he can count up to five.

"He has a badly turned eye. We're waiting for him to see a specialist."

That explains the jigsaw situation. Perhaps he will be sent off to see a specialist very soon, hopefully during my Teaching Practice.

"Now the girls. There are sixteen of them."

A quick calculation tells me that shockingly there are thirty-five little bodies in this classroom. That's it: that's the extra ingredient to the aroma. In fact, there is more than one extra. The smells consist of a few cleanly washed heads of hair and several which are not, together with some newly washed jumpers and a few which haven't seen the inside of a washing machine for weeks. All mixed together with the pencils and the paper to give that unique school smell.

The room looks crowded. Thirty-five is too many. How can it be possible to get to know all of them? Not only do I have to learn their names, but all about each one, what they are capable of and importantly, what they are not capable of doing.

Mrs Hudson continues in her smooth, efficient-sounding voice with more words of experience.

"Classes that are heavy on the number of boys are always the toughest."

I smile weakly. Really? Just my luck.

Then she whispers in a confidential tone, "See the girl colouring in on the table at the back, the one with her hair in bunches?"

I nod, but say nothing. At this stage, I'm not sure I'm supposed to be making comments.

"You need to be aware she is short-tongued. It makes sounding out words with a letter 's', a bit difficult for her. But I wouldn't worry too much. It's early days."

I feel certain that I will worry about it. How will she manage a simple sentence? What about, 'The thun ith in the thky', for instance? It'll be impossible for her to spell.

But my class teacher isn't finished. She has more information to impart, all sounding like bad news to me.

"And the little girl next to her? The one wiping her nose across her sleeve?"

I nod again. Once more that nauseating feeling rises up. Stronger than when I beheld my fried egg this morning.

"She hardly speaks at all. I doubt if you'll get anything out of her. Not in speech and certainly not in writing. She'll no doubt end up at a special school."

No doubt. Now I know I definitely do not want to teach at a special school. Are there any normal children in this class, I wonder?

As if to put me out of my spiralling descent into misery, Mrs Hudson closes the register and assumes a brisker tone of voice. "Now, if you'd like to bring up a chair, I'll get the children to come and sit round so I can introduce you."

With the least apparent effort, she stands up, stops the class going about their activities, orders books to be put away tidily and jigsaws to be stacked on the correct shelves in the correct cupboards.

Quietly and to my eyes miraculously, after two or three minutes, desks now cleared, the children take their places on the floor in front of their waiting teacher, legs crossed, eyes uplifted. Even the neglected, attention-seeking child and the boy with the turned eye melt into the whole group.

Producing a large scrapbook, seemingly from nowhere, Mrs Hudson begins to turn its pages and reads out short poems and rhymes to the assembled class. At intervals she turns the pages round to face them, so that they can see the pictures. The children are entranced. Sometimes they just listen, their mouths open, their eyes wide; sometimes they join in with all the words.

Their teacher tells her eager listeners how she has been collecting all these little favourites over her many years of teaching. Silently I vow to begin such a book for my future pupils. I should begin right away, the sooner the better. Perhaps tonight. In the meantime, I know I hold no such fascinating attraction. My newly bought *Puffin Book of Verses* will have to do.

At last the moment arrives when my name is announced. All eyes swivel to the small person sitting at the front on one of their chairs. I hear Mrs Hudson tell them that I am to be their teacher for the next five weeks. Feeling less than ever like a member of that esteemed profession whose ranks I am attempting to join, I give the children the best smile I can manage. Friendly, but not too friendly. Cheerful on the outside, fearful on the inside.

At the back of my mind, I think about all those schemes of work I have so carefully thought out at College. Am I capable of carrying them out? Have I catered adequately for a boy with a turned eye and a girl who never speaks? The task ahead is immense.

Tuesday morning. To look more like the part I have to play, I stand in front of the mirror in our tiny shared bedroom, a bunch of hairclips in my hand. With sweeps of the brush, I pin my long hair up into a neat bun. Looking with satisfaction at my reflection, I decide that today, I must become Miss Hardy.

CHAPTER TWENTY-FIVE

~~~

A FAILURE
TO IMPRESS

"Now children, shake your hands high up in the air… and low down near the floor, while I rattle my tambourine."

The class, in bare feet and dressed in pants and vests in various shades of white right through to unwashed grey, spring into action. It has already taken the best part of a quarter of an hour after the end of playtime to supervise the removal of trousers, shirts, cardigans, skirts, shoes and socks. Although I had stressed that their clothes should be left in neat piles and a sock pushed into each shoe, I had to abandon that ambition while I supervised the untying of laces and the unfastening of buttons. The classroom resembles the stage set of a war zone. I'm already exhausted before the actual lesson begins.

Hands fling wildly anywhere: in front of neighbours' faces, round ears and behind bottoms. The contortions are endless. For the most part, my pupils are ignoring the tambourine rattling and instead, inventing their own rhythms.

Miss Watson, my tutor, here to observe and to give helpful criticism, writes secretly in her notebook and then looks up to give me an encouraging smile. I decide swift action is required.

"Stop everyone. And stand very still with hands by sides."

It works. I have learned something in my PE lectures, although there are still two or three miscreants continuing to flap their hands about.

Time for the 'climax' of the lesson. I had worked it out, cleverly I thought, late last night. This ought to impress her, a dance specialist at that. And me, one of her most enthusiastic students, to boot. What could go wrong?

"Children who sit at the red table, go and stand over there." I point across the hall to my left, only half-noticing out of the corner of my eye the musical instrument trolley.

"But we're not sitting at our tables. We're in the hall," pipes up a helpful voice.

"I know we are. I mean, those who usually sit at the red table, go and stand over there," I repeat patiently.

About six of them trundle across and proceed to hang over and lean on the trolley.

"Now, those who sit at the blue table, stand in that corner."

I point in the opposite direction, towards a pile of gym mats.

"I only sometimes sit at the blue table," interrupts a member of the awkward squad. "Sometimes you put me by the window to work by myself."

I continue to speak slowly and carefully. "Well, you *belong* on the blue table. So, you go with them."

The red table children are now poking the castanets and making sly jiggles of the tambourines. I had better hurry things up.

"The yellow table people stand over there." I point to the third corner.

"And the orange table…"

"Then what do we do?" shouts a freckly-faced boy with shockingly ginger hair. He starts hopping from foot to foot. "Can we play 'Farmer's in his Den'? That's what we do with Mrs Hudson."

"Well, I'm not Mrs Hudson," I say firmly. "We're not playing 'Farmer's in his Den', we're …orange table, you should be over there."

"But you never said where."

"What about us?"

"Which corner shall we stand in?"

I realise with dismay that I have another tableful of children to dispense with and no more corners. I frantically try to distribute the remaining group to make the numbers equal.

By now, there is a cacophony of sound from the music trolley end and a lot of leaping and bouncing going on at the other side on top of the gym mats. The yellow table corner are attempting to organise their own version of 'Farmer's in his Den', arguing over who should be the farmer. The orange table are rolling all over the beautifully polished parquet floor in the middle of the hall.

I feebly clap my hands. What little discipline I had in the first place is rapidly dissipating. I hurry across to the record player, where my 'Carnival of the Animals' LP is ready on the turntable. I hover the needle over the exact track, entitled 'The Swan'. This climax could be so successful.

"When you hear the music, slowly move into the middle ..."

"Where's the middle?"

"Mrs Hudson never plays us music."

I give a withered, defeated look at Miss Watson, a silent appeal for help. What is the use of me being any good at dance, if I cannot gain the children's attention, to even begin? It is so disappointing.

My tutor, in her regulation neat white collar, pleated skirt and laced-up gym shoes, sweeps over towards me and whispers with authority and her rather too plum accent.

"Don't you worry, my dear, I'll take over from here."

As Miss Watson steps forward, the class immediately becomes quiet, all eyes upon this tall, unknown figure with an unfamiliar voice. The question is written on their faces. What is she going to tell them to do?

She stretches out her hand to demand the tambourine. I give it to her gratefully and step back with utter relief, ready to watch carefully and see her method.

Her voice sounds loud and carrying, each word spoken slowly and clearly.

"I'm going to bang the tambourine and you make big stamps on the floor, all around."

And Miss Watson is certainly a sight to be seen: an old girls' grammar school type with silver-grey hair, cut very short in almost masculine style. She rattles the tambourine wildly. The children whoop as they leap around the hall.

As she moves nearer towards me, she says, "This will get it out of their systems." I nod matter-of-factly, as if I knew that all along.

Then my esteemed tutor stops suddenly and lowers the tambourine almost to the floor. She also lowers her voice on her next command. "Now, tiptoe round and be like little mice."

She follows her own instruction, but to my horror, no one else does. The children continue to stamp and make as much noise as they were doing before. Perhaps it's because they have not heard this second instruction. Or perhaps she did not speak Teesside.

That's it. They don't understand her educated accent.

"Come on now. LITTLE MICE," she urges, more loudly this time.

But it is no use. Not one little mouse is to be found among them.

Somehow or other, the defeated Miss Watson ushers them all back into the retreat of the classroom. Following the children across the hall with me, she says in confidential tones, "Now I can understand what problems you are facing, my dear."

Far from going down in my estimation, I admire her even more. My climax had failed. But then, so had she.

CHAPTER TWENTY-SIX

~~~~

A LIGHT AT THE END
OF THE TUNNEL

Every day, after the children have left the building in a whirlwind of hats, coats, scarves and gloves, clutching reading books and soggy paintings, Penny and I spend at least an hour mounting pictures and displaying them carefully on the walls of the classroom. We've had endless art lectures on choosing colours, getting the margins right and lining up work in an artistic manner. Then there's the printing to be completed: it must be neat, every letter carefully formed in lower case with larger capitals. The 'a's must be perfectly round and the 'l's must be perfectly straight. Exhausting, but necessary.

Then it's a slow walk back to digs, each of us loaded with bags which are full of more work to be completed before we can even think of taking a rest.

Mrs Stewart's usually large and hefty tea revives us somewhat. Our cooked breakfasts are now reduced to a bacon sandwich or perhaps scrambled eggs on toast, gently requested by us and much more suited to our queasy, morning stomachs. But in the evening, we demolish all that is laid before us. School does give you a ferocious appetite.

Once the plates are cleared away, we set to work at the kitchen table on our mammoth task. We must analyse today's lessons, prepare work cards for tomorrow, enough for the various groups of children, and add the final touches to the next lot of lesson plans. We must cut out, glue and stick and label anything and everything. As the time nears ten o'clock, we pack our bags ready for the morning, dive into the shower or take a quick plunge in and out of the bath before finally rolling into our narrow single beds to snatch a few hours of sleep.

My trusty alarm clock rudely awakens us ridiculously early, and we force ourselves out from under the warm blankets to get up and start all over again. And each morning, as I attempt to clean my teeth, that feeling of trepidation about the day ahead is still causing me to retch over the basin.

There is no let up, no ease from the pressure between Monday morning and Friday evening. We never look at a newspaper, see a television screen, read a novel, discuss anything that is not to do with teaching children.

It is a small relief when the College coach arrives at the bottom of the street at the end of the week. We collapse into the seats and once more make contact with our friends. Only then can we laugh with each other about our silly mistakes and tell tales about the children who misbehaved, the stories that ended in disaster and the PE lessons that dissolved into thin air.

We are let out. There are almost two whole days to look forward to, getting back to being ourselves at College.

Once in Bishopsfield, Penny leaves us to go across town to her college flat while Alison and I trudge down the bank with our cases to Northgate. It's dark and damp in the autumn air and we think about the milky coffee and iced buns Mrs Parker will have put out for us for supper. It's always there when we get in, as if by magic. We never actually see anyone place it on the table. No one says "Goodnight girls" or "Sweet dreams, ladies". Perhaps there is a secret robot who senses when it is safe to come out of the kitchen and then disappears again. However, the coffee and buns or scones, or whatever delicious morsel we find on a plate are always very welcome.

With Northgate in sight, Alison sets out her plan for the evening ahead. "First, it's a nice chat with Jill and Brenda while we eat our supper and then bed for me. I've borrowed this mindless magazine off someone on the bus."

We dump our cases in the hallway and fling open the

study room door, ready to spring onto Jill and Brenda with a massive cheer to show we are so glad to be back. But the place is dark and the gas fire turned off. Far from being a cosy retreat with friends eager and waiting to hear all our news, the room is cold and cheerless.

Switching on the light, we see a note on the table:

Dear Alison and Amelia,

Got an offer of a lift home to Bradford, so couldn't miss the chance. Brenda's getting the 6 o'clock bus tonight as she's remembered it's her dad's birthday tomorrow. Enjoy yourselves. See you next weekend.

Love Jill Xx

"Great. Just great." Alison flops down into the nearest armchair. I drop the note into the wastepaper basket. The little balloon of elation we felt on the coach journey back is truly and completely deflated.

Like a recurring bad dream, Sunday afternoon turns up with sickening regularity, and here we are on the coach heading due north-east for Thornberry. It's like being lashed onto a tortuous treadmill. Once Penny and I set foot in the Stewarts' household, it's back to the grindstone, similar to my teenage diary: school, homework, bed. Nothing else happens.

Teaching two groups for number and writing is all that's required of us at this stage and I'm finding it fairly well within my capabilities. Looming at the back of my mind though is the fact that there are another three groups to be taught. Once qualified, I shall have to deal with those numbers of children. When it comes to lessons 'en masse' on the other hand, like PE, RE and Music, the entirety of the class has to be managed and like the climax of my last attempt at a Dance lesson, is proving to be difficult to get right.

I do have one weapon in my armoury which gives me confidence. After enduring years of elocution training, which lots of people do these days to get rid of their regional accents, I know how to read a story out loud, how to use an interesting voice and keep eye contact with my listeners. So, once my class is in front of me, there is some satisfaction in being in the classroom with thirty-five pairs of eyes and ears.

It's a different problem I am wrestling with before the story can begin: how to get the children to pick up every single last piece of jigsaw, building brick and cutting-out paper. How to get them to put away the scissors, stack the Plasticine boards and be ready sitting on the floor for story time before the bell for home-time rings.

The problem doesn't stop there. If it's raining, all the children's coats have to be fastened, gloves located and sometimes wellies changed into before they shuffle into some semblance of an orderly line, ready to be led out to their waiting mothers. I am often beaten by the clock, so my thirty-five little charges are never ready by the time the bell rings at half past three.

My tutor can say nothing that helps, and watching Mrs Hudson merely serves to highlight my inexperience. Every day I try and every day sees some sort of disaster. My role as 'Miss Hardy' is not yet perfected. Even my carefully pinned bun in my hair doesn't help.

Today I see a tiny flicker of light at the end of my long dark tunnel. It appears in the form of a letter from my mother. She writes one every other day without fail, and I generally keep my message from home until late in the evening. Penny looks on, hoping that I will read out the amusing bits, as she never receives any post at all.

It's been a dismal, wet Monday. The children haven't been able to get outside to play at all and true to form, I've spent ages before home-time matching up pairs of wellies. So Mam's letter is more than usually welcome, especially when I read out the part where she tells me my sister and brother-in-law are planning to drive her down after school later this week. Thursday, in fact. The venue is to be a huge supermarket on the outskirts of Thornberry which sells everything under the sun, all under one roof.

This is happy news on two counts. Firstly, I shall see my lovely family, even if it's just for a couple of hours. Secondly, such a huge establishment is a novelty. My mother does all her shopping the traditional way:

bread from the baker's, fruit and vegetables from the greengrocer's and meat from the butcher's. I remember Fran telling us about Sainsbury's when I remarked on her brand of toothpaste. I'd never heard of it.

The little supermarket in Bishopsfield where we do our bit of student-type shopping is tiny. It does live up to its name though. It's called 'Usave', with the letters displayed outside vertically, and we can buy digestives or custard creams for a mere shilling a packet. It means that three pounds can be spun out over a whole week. Just.

Meanwhile, the thought of our little outing to this massive shop keeps me spiritually alive all through the next day and the next. I reckon Penny and I are due for an evening off. She tells me she's looking forward to seeing my family again, after meeting them a few times in Dale House.

We catch the bus into town, meet Mam, Judith and Pete and head straight for the restaurant, which is also under this immense warehouse of a shop. Over coffee and a huge piece of chocolate cake my big sister, a veteran teacher of five years, gives us some moral support. Penny and I are assured that the second Teaching Practice is the hardest and things are sure to come right eventually.

Feeling outwardly cheered on the journey back to digs, I still have my private doubts, wondering if I am ever to find my inner 'Miss Hardy'.

On Friday morning, events take a turn which horrifies

me. My worst nightmare is about to begin, the very one I prayed would never happen. But happening it is, right now.

CHAPTER TWENTY-SEVEN

~~~

MY INNER
MISS HARDY

Mrs Hudson has not yet arrived at school. There's been no word from her. Every morning previously, she's been here in the classroom by eight o'clock and now it's half past.

My lesson plans only include the whole class for the first half an hour. After that, I've prepared as usual for my own two groups, the red table and the blue table. What are the other three to do? If Mrs Hudson doesn't appear, I hope and pray fervently that the headmistress will take over. I'm slightly in awe of her and haven't exchanged much more than a few sentences since we first arrived.

Quarter to nine and I'm beginning to panic. Mrs Finlay sends a message with one of the juniors that

I must report to her office. I scoot along to the door, appropriately labelled 'Headmistress', knock and enter. With a detached, official air and no hint of a smile, she informs me that she has an important meeting and could I possibly cope, just until playtime. Mrs Hudson has telephoned to say she would try her best to get into school by then. No explanation of her absence is given.

I close the door behind me and take a deep breath. I remember the advice pummelled into me at home. Shoulders back, chin up. I tell myself, of course I can manage. Failure and cowardice have never been part of my vocabulary. If you don't like something, you don't just give up. Well, apart from tap dancing, which only lasted three weeks. But that doesn't count. I was only eight at the time.

No, I have given much thought to this, my chosen career. I am not about to falter at the first hurdle. This is a crisis and I want to show I can be counted upon when I am needed. The class requires a teacher and here I am, practising to be one. This is it.

Wake up Miss Hardy!

As I walk back to the classroom, I feel a calmness descend upon me. With Mrs Hudson not around at all, not even hovering in the background as she has been wont to do, I know it is up to me to make any decisions. I am the teacher today, I will tell them all what to do, I will say when to tidy up, when to go out to play.

I have to think quickly. For the three groups not

planned for, I find some work cards in a drawer and decide to set the children off working on these, first making sure that the concept is not new to them. There are enough number games and reading apparatus around the room to keep them busy after they finish their allotted task.

At nine o'clock, when my thirty-five little bodies take their seats on their miniature wooden chairs, I am the person sitting at the teacher's desk with the open register and the red pen. For the very first time, I hear those thrilling words after I call out each name:

"Yes, Miss Hardy".

And in that large book, which I had peered at with some trepidation on my first day here, I put a diagonal red line in each little square to denote each child's presence. It is peculiar how it is the little things which make one feel like a proper teacher.

"Yes, you may borrow the rubber from my desk."

"Yes, you may sharpen your pencil."

All these little trifles have previously been dealt with by Mrs Hudson. Because the children are now referring to me and no one else, I feel completely in charge.

The first half of the morning runs smoothly. I tell my RE story to the whole class, who, to my surprise, all listen with rapt attention. The sets of work cards are distributed and worked through. I patrol the desks and scribe large, red ticks with a thick, felt pen, adding smiley faces beside the children's best efforts. Even the tidying away part is achieved without mishap. When the bell rings, I feel great satisfaction in hearing myself say, "Right, you may go out to play now", and then I send them out table by table to collect their coats, so that they don't all scamper out at once. And it works.

Back in the staffroom during playtime, I am given the bad news that would have sent me into a breath-taking panic, had I heard it yesterday. Mrs Hudson won't be coming in at all today. Tragically, her grown-up son has been involved in a motorbike accident and been rushed into hospital. His injuries are worse than was first thought and she must stay with him.

The crisis is real.

When the bell for lessons rings I walk back across the hall, sounding the heels of my shoes. I am ready to greet 'my' class as they hurtle in after play. No longer do their ever-moving arms and legs seem like an uncontrollable mass. They whirl into the classroom with bright eyes and glowing cheeks, bringing the smell of the cold air with them and flinging coats and hats onto pegs in the porch. Order cannot be restored until a bevy of agitators are listened to, insistent upon claiming their right to attention. Mrs Hudson usually spends quite a few minutes sorting out playtime problems. Today, I am in the firing line.

"Miss, Richard won't give me my ball back."

"Look, I fell down and I've got some cream on my knee."

"I didn't have time to go to the toilet before the bell. Can I go now?"

At my intervention, Richard gives Susan her ball back, Michael proudly shows his creamed knee to the rest of his table and Steven disappears out to the toilet, having been told firmly by me to 'Be quick". As he shuts the door behind him, the rest of the class, most of whom are already sitting in their seats, swivel their eyes towards me. I tell the others who are dithering around to hurry up and sit down, thinking at the same time I will write a story on the board with the help of the whole class.

"Susan and Tracy, give out the writing books, please."

And I turn, pick up a long, smooth stick of white chalk and write in my best, very large, printed letters on the blackboard: 'My Family'. A subject close to my own heart.

Miss Hardy is beginning to teach at last.

CHAPTER TWENTY-EIGHT

~~~~

DECEMBER 1970

THE END OF OLD TRADITIONS

Teaching Practice is over. The pressure's off. So in the dark evenings and during the wet weekends, how do we amuse ourselves, the four of us cooped up in our little room in Northgate?

Describing one of our activities as singing songs may be a slight exaggeration, as I'm still in the early stages of learning to play the guitar that Mam picked up for me during half-term, second-hand. So far, I've graduated from two to three chords, which is a major step forward. Holding down the relevant strings, once I find them, is not so much of a problem; it's changing from chord to chord which is the tricky bit. Jill, Alison and Brenda are press-ganged into being my participating audience, while we painfully sing my current favourite folk song, complete with pauses.

"*I'll give to you,*" pause to change chord, "*a paper of pins,*" pause, "*'cos that's the way my,*" pause, "*love begins,*" pause. And so on through all four verses.

It'll come in useful for my next Teaching Practice, I tell them, when I'm more proficient.

"And when it doesn't take half an hour to sing one song," grumbles Brenda.

To prove we still haven't quite finished with childhood just yet, we invent bizarre games that turn the normal world upside down. This is what comes from having little money, no television and more than enough imagination. Working with young children might also have something to do with it. You catch their acute awareness and enthusiasm, look at everything afresh and see things with new eyes.

During the weekends, my red Dansette record player, another second-hand acquisition, is a frequent feature of our entertainment. It plays singles and LPs in mono and the extent of its power ranges from turning the volume up or down. The hours of pleasure derived from this humble machine are endless. One of my newly acquired records, a birthday present from my grandmother, is of two pianists with an orchestral backing, playing a medley of every well-known classic from Beethoven's serene 'Moonlight Sonata' to Rachmaninov's dramatic 'Rhapsody'.

In a spirit of wild abandonment, we spend a whole evening miming to this record: Alison on piano, Jill sawing away furiously on strings, Brenda improvising on all the other instruments, while I act the role of conductor. Our arms fling about while the wonderful music plays in concert style. Alison dips imaginary sizzling red-hot fingers into an imaginary bucket of cold water, Jill fiddles furiously and Brenda leaps from cymbals to trumpets, while I beat time in the air with a wooden ruler. If Mrs P should happen to open the hatch doors, we would make a peculiar spectacle. But no doubt she imagines we must be sitting and quietly taking in the beauty of the classical pieces, because that is all that can be heard. If only she knew what was going on, silently, on the other side of her kitchen wall!

Next morning, my arms ache terribly.

Our musical evenings come to an abrupt halt when one day the lights go out. Not just ours in Northgate, but the whole of College and the town of Bishopsfield. We finally get hold of a newspaper and find out it isn't just our local area, but most of the country. There's a work-to-rule going on, as all workers clamour for pay rises and the nation's electricity has to be cut off at certain times of the day.

We are getting used to candle-lit dinners in digs. They are probably a nightmare for Mrs P, but a source of amusement for us immature souls. It begins as an excitement, but with each repeat performance, the novelty wears thin.

"It's all the Government's fault," Alison moans as she dips her rationed one slice of bread into the soup: there are never any 'seconds' forthcoming.

"That is not the correct way," I remonstrate. "This is how you do it." And I wipe the back of my soup spoon onto a corner of my own slice of bread.

"Well, it's only you sitting opposite, not the Queen," says Alison.

"We can't see anything anyway," Jill points out, "Not by the light of a couple of candles."

"Perhaps that's a good thing," says Brenda, between spoonfuls of the lukewarm liquid. "I don't fancy looking too closely at this soup. There might be great globules of fat floating about."

Jill is having none of it. "It tastes all right, and that's all I'm bothered about." Then she begins moaning, which isn't like her. "If the electricity folk would only get themselves back to work, everyone wouldn't have to suffer. I couldn't even have a shower this afternoon up at College. No hot water."

"But Mr Heath won't relent," says Alison. "In fact, I think he should give them what they're asking for."

"Why should he?" I reply. "The unions are holding the country to ransom." That's what I read on the Comments page in last Sunday's paper and I repeat the powerful phrase with a certain satisfaction.

Alison agrees. "And another thing – I'm sick of not getting any letters. Don't understand why we have to put up with a postal strike at the same time."

Brenda says she doesn't care because it saves us the bother of having to write.

Our political debate is interrupted by the sound of the hatch doors opening. Brenda springs into action, balancing a pile of empty soup dishes in one hand and catching the first dinner plate with the other.

It's always the same. No words spoken with the appearance of our meals. We're used to it now. Our evening dinner in front of us and the hatch doors safely closed, Alison whispers, "She didn't even ask us how we're managing with our candles".

"I suppose we didn't ask her how she'd managed to cook it," I say, philosophically.

Brenda looks pityingly at me.

"She managed because she's got a gas cooker, you daft thing!"

The approach to Christmas inevitably draws our minds towards presents, with the same problem as last year: what to buy with the few pennies we have left in our banks.

However, some welcome news comes our way. Several weeks after the end of Teaching Practice, we hear that a sum of money is owed to each one of us. Apparently, a miscalculation was made on the number of school dinners we consumed and paid for. Like turning over a lucky Chance card in Monopoly, we are to receive the princely sum of £3 each, like manna from heaven. A shopping spree is called for.

After our usual rummage round the market picking up bargains, a silky scarf here and a tin of biscuits there, it's towards the end of the afternoon when we head back through the darkening streets. The four of us are full of Christmas spirit, our bags loaded with the cheapest gifts we've been able to find. Without the aid of street lights, switched off early because of the strikes, we make our way towards Woolworth's, our last port of call.

Entering that high street establishment to pick up our last-minute odds and ends, we find, as we push open the double doors, a great surprise. The old-fashioned shop with its original dark wooden counters is dimly lit by its own gas lamps, still intact and hanging on chains from the ceiling. We feel we have stepped back in time and had a glimpse into the past, the not so very distant past when things and people looked so different in the soft, mellow gaslight. The only thing that hasn't changed is the prices. Our £3 budget remains firmly in 1970.

It's early December. Too early. That is, too early for the end of term. But a notice signed by her Majesty the Principal herself announces that due to the continuing electricity cuts, all students are to be sent down for the Christmas vacation two weeks ahead of schedule.

It's ridiculous, we wail. Why? Why should we return to our darkened homes? We prefer to stay in darkness here.

Then the second notice goes up. This is a more crushing blow. There is to be no Second Year Review and no Formal Christmas Dinner.

These are two long-standing traditions at St Mag's. The first is a comedy appraisal of life in College, showcasing its most eccentric lecturers. The second is a moving affair which we experienced in our first year, involving, ironically, eating dinner by candlelight – a way of life we have grown accustomed to – and the singing of carols in the dining hall before the meal is served. Formally.

We are acutely aware that these two traditions thereafter will die. Come next Christmas, the majority of students will have no knowledge of them and so, as is the way of life, things will move on and never return. No appeal is granted. We are to be sent home without ceremony and without any festive memories.

Except one.

This is entirely within our own initiative. No Principal is going to sit on this tradition. It's unwritten, unspoken, kept strictly secret and organised by quiet whispers in corners.

It's half past five in the morning, our last morning before we are all to go home. It isn't exactly Christmas Eve, but it's December and that makes it all right.

As instructed, we drag ourselves from our alluring warm beds to stagger in pitch blackness up the hill to College and across the path between the lawns. Under the horse chestnut tree we can just make out a crowd of students, pinpricked by torchlights and at one end, a lantern held high. Voices are low and muffled in the damp, morning air. Dressed for the cold in woolly hats, mitts and thick College scarves, we walk across the wet grass to join the waiting group. Then, as one body, we all move away from the lawn towards College, quietly singing 'Silent Night'. It is our turn to be the angel voices singing to the sleeping first years, as happened to us last Christmas.

As I link arms with Jill to follow the swinging lantern, I reflect on how far I have come since then: learning not only how to be a teacher but also about myself.

The first years peer bleary-eyed round their bedroom doors, wondering what is happening, just as we did. This time last December, everything was still new and bewildering. And I think of how, since then, new friends have been made, some friends lost on the way and a family of good friends has been created. I have taken a step nearer that world of school I have chosen to enter. And somehow, in order to find success, I did find strength within. There are many more steps to take and there's going to be more inner strength to find.

But for now, I put all that aside and think only of the moment as we join hands around the horse chestnut tree to sing 'Auld Lang Syne' as the darkness fades and the sky lightens.

CHAPTER TWENTY-NINE

~~~

FEBRUARY 1971

THE LURE OF THE COUNTRYSIDE

"Are you coming, Jill?" I peer round our study room door. "Hurry up. We're setting off in a minute to walk to Royal Grange Park. And the sun's just come out."

She looks up for a moment from a thick tome. "No thanks. Think I'll give it a miss."

I don't mind. We all feel free to decide for ourselves. I've come to realise that sometimes, Jill is quite content with her own company and I don't try to persuade her, as experience has taught me that this would be a fruitless exercise. I let her get back to *War and Peace*, which is Jill's idea of reading for pleasure. I'm far more attracted to this novel idea of 'going for a walk', never having known this kind of leisure pursuit.

At home growing up, if you went out, it was for some particular purpose, like running the messages, which means going to the shops with a shopping list. Or perhaps visiting someone, usually an aunty or our grandmother. It was referred to as 'calling' at their house. 'I'm going to call at Aunty Alice's', we would say. And yes, that might mean getting on the bus there and walking back, but specifically 'going for a walk'? Never.

Alison and I have started these outings every Sunday afternoon with Helen and Becky, two new friends I am just getting to know this year from our main English group. Helen happens to be one of the few students who come from Cumbria. Of this she is very proud and she can often be heard extolling the virtues of her native town, never letting us forget that it is set in the foothills of the wonderful Lake District. In her eyes, the flat-ish fields around Bishopsfield come a poor second best.

On the other hand, I'm just discovering the countryside. Until now, living by the sea has always been a priority for where I might live in the future. What scenery could rival that strip of blue on the horizon, its depth of colour changing with the seasons and the weather?

But gradually the greenery of Yorkshire is slowly winning me over. And so I look forward to our weekly jaunts into the countryside. Although the air is holding on to that late winter nip, we tell ourselves that spring is just around the corner.

Helen and Becky are waiting for me and Alison in the hallway. I first met Becky, who happens to be another old school friend of Alison's, one Saturday morning last term in 'non-res wash room'. Hours are spent in that basement in College, slopping woollies and sitting on the spin dryer to stop it from dancing around the smooth lino.

That particular day, as we descended the stone steps with bags full of laundry, I heard someone singing Joni Mitchell's song 'Both Sides Now'. Becky stood alone at one of the huge sinks, rubbing out and rinsing in the steam and the aroma of soap flakes. Her voice floated up to the high ceiling and echoed around the vast walls of white tiles. She sang about 'ice cream castles in the air' and 'feather canyons everywhere'. I have no idea what the words mean, but it doesn't matter. They hold a certain dreamy attraction and surely must belong to the same school of music which invites us to sing to lampposts, as in 'I've come to watch your flowers growing'. I can feel the optimism of the 1960s is still very much with us as we march on into the next decade.

And so Becky's singing cheered us up that day when we were all weighed down by the hard slog of Teaching Practice.

Now we are about to set off, the four of us, for some much-needed fresh but chilly spring air. We are suitably dressed in duffel coats and thick, green College scarves with their distinctive cream stripes. At the last minute, I remember my new woollen Arran beret, my Christmas present from Mam, and then have to hurry to catch up with the other three, tramping down Mrs P's garden path.

"Look, the goldfish are frozen over." Alison steps onto the lawn to poke at the icy pond water with a twig. "Jill hasn't done her duty today."

"What duty?" asks Helen.

"Well, every morning as we go out and every evening when we get back from lectures, she cracks the ice to make a few breathing holes for the goldfish. You would never believe it, during the winter Mrs P leaves the fish out here and brings the gnomes inside."

"I wondered what they were doing in the hallway," Helen giggles. "I nearly fell over them."

We cross the road and make our way out of town, lured towards the wide open spaces of the countryside.

"Let's take the path across the fields," I suggest. "At least, it's too frosty at the moment to be muddy."

When we come to a signpost that says 'ROYAL GRANGE PARK - 2 MILES', we open a squeaky, iron gate leading to a winding footpath. It's perfect weather for walking: no wind, a glint of early afternoon sunshine through the bare trees and just cold enough to make our noses turn red.

Helen is the serious and sober type. Sober in the well-balanced, self-possessed meaning of the word. If Alison and I get into a giddy mood, she can act as if she is our maiden aunt advising irresponsible children. The rest of us think that one day she will become a proper career girl and make a fine headmistress. But this afternoon, there is no silliness, no laughing about not very much until our sides ache. Nothing which Helen can admonish us about. There is a serious subject to discuss. There's been trouble brewing in digs.

And so, we talk while we walk.

Our two friends haven't been happy since last September and lately, they tell us that things have gone from bad to worse. Becky describes the minute portions their landlady serves up for tea and the awful mixtures of things, like one tiny beef burger and a spoonful of soggy cabbage: as she points out, not enough to feed a fly, let alone students who are permanently hungry. We all curl our noses up in disgust. It sounds even worse than our greasy pies.

Trudging along, hands in pockets to keep warm, we laugh about their one-bar electric fire. Alison and I agree how fortunate we are in Northgate, despite our gas fire permanently set to miser rate and our meals shoved through the hatch like a conveyor belt.

"Ours is a palace compared to yours," Alison says. "Although we do grumble when Mrs P vacuums right up to our bedroom doors every Saturday morning at eight o'clock. I'm sure it's on purpose, to make us get up."

I point out to our friends the one silver lining: that they are soon to be given rooms in College. But both Becky and Helen insist that they'd rather have decent digs.

As we turn into the avenue of trees which leads to the park, the conversation changes to where we might live in the third year, although nothing has to be decided until next term. Alison and I explain that we have our sights set on the most modern Hall of Residence: to have a room to yourself with your own handbasin would be a thing most wonderful. Luxury indeed! Beechwood House will definitely be top of our list.

Royal Grange is reached at last and the park looks beautiful with the sun shining on the lake and a little family of ducks paddling round in expectation of visitors with crusts of bread. We sit on a bench, share a couple of bars of chocolate and ruminate about our future, until we realise the afternoon is turning too chilly to stay still for long and it's time to get walking again.

On our way back across the fields, the roofline of Bishopsfield visible in the distance, we make plans to continue our afternoon walks and to visit all the little villages hereabouts right though into the summer, maybe have a picnic in the warmer weather. I insist it has to be a proper one with a tablecloth spread out on the grass, like in all the best Enid Blyton stories. The picnics of my childhood were always on the beach with the taste of gritty sand in our sandwiches and the feel of the salty wind whipping up our damp hair and on goose-pimpled arms.

In this newly discovered countryside, I can feel the fresh air, the exercise and the break from studying doing us all an immense power of good. Not only all of those things, but also the talking, the continual talking: supporting each other and setting out our dreams for the future. We all want to teach in a country school, make a difference in some children's lives, and not least, find love with exactly the right person.

But none of us can ever know exactly what may be out there waiting for us.

CHAPTER THIRTY

~~~

JUNE 1971

A WEEK IN WET WALES

It is all organised. A week in sunny France.

My penfriend and I have been writing to each other for about the last eight years. It has done wonders to improve my French. I always used to sit at the front of the class for these lessons, shooting up my hand to answer most of the questions, alert and eager: unlike Maths and Chemistry, when I would try to slither down my seat to escape notice.

Earlier this summer, the longed-for invitation arrived. Maryse, my French penfriend, asked me to stay with her for a whole week. Continental travel. How exotic that sounds! To put it mildly, I am high with excitement.

In an unusual shopping spree during the summer half-term, Mam and I picked out a couple of new blouses and a cotton skirt at the little dress shop she frequents, where she is friendly with the manageress. More to the point, Mam has an account there, so that payment can be arranged in instalments. She says I need to look half decent during my French holiday, and I'm expecting the weather to be a teensy bit warmer than down the beach back at home. There are only the travel arrangements still to be sorted out and by some miracle, we have scraped together enough for the train fare.

After all these years, at last I'll be able to try out my well-practised, '*Bonjour, Maryse! Comment allez vous?*'

It's a sunny June morning at the breakfast table in Northgate and I can hardly wait to open my post, as I see that one of the two items is an envelope addressed in Maryse's very French-looking handwriting. Meanwhile Alison is busy dishing out the cornflakes, Jill collects the toast before it falls out of the hatch and Brenda pours the tea for the four of us.

I put aside the one which is obviously Mam's letter and slit open the envelope, unmistakably French with its flowery, foreign stamps.

Brenda puts down the teapot. "What's the matter?"

"She's having difficulty translating the French," scoffs Alison.

"No I am not," I answer back firmly. "Anyway, Maryse has deigned to write this all in English."

"Well, go on. Is it something about your holiday?" asks Jill.

I look up from the letter. "I just can't believe it. It's all off."

"Off? Why?"

"The long and the short of it is she's getting married. Not only that, but she's expecting a baby." I push the letter back into the envelope and toss it across the table. "Apparently she's just found out she's pregnant, so it's a rush wedding in the summer. And that's why my visit is out." I take a sip of hot tea and almost burn my mouth. "Oh, and she suggests one day I can come over with *my* husband. Highly likely, I must say!"

I butter a slice of toast vehemently. "So, no France for me, this year, or probably ever."

"Good!" says Alison.

I look at her in amazement. Am I not to receive any sympathy? But Alison looks as if she has just had a great idea.

"Now you can come with us to sunny Wales instead. Pass the sugar, please."

It's been a long haul from the railway station in pouring rain, with each of us loaded down with a suitcase and bags. Our 'highly desirable' holiday flat, as it was described in the advertisement, turns out to be up three flights of stairs. I suppose the 'desirable' part means that we are situated right on the front with views of the rather grey looking sea.

Weary and dripping wet, we drop our luggage on the landing and step inside our front door. The flat opens directly and unexpectedly into the kitchen. The description we have been given told us in glowing terms of the view of the mountains from the back. True, as we peer out of the sash window, we can see a slight rise of green above a range of roofs and chimney pots, but mountains? Hardly.

A surprising feature of the kitchen is, that it boasts a double bed, the foot of which ends at the side of the fridge. Someone is destined to enjoy cold feet for a week, and I hope it's not me. The front bedroom (there is no living room) holds two double beds, a washbasin (wonderful) and a view of the seafront (better than the so-called 'view of the mountains' at the back).

By some collective decision, Helen, Alison, Jill and I are the fortunate occupiers of this bedroom. Brenda and a friend of hers from schooldays make up the fifth and sixth members of our little holiday group. They have lost the toss and must sleep in the kitchen.

By no means could this be described as a luxury flat, but we're not going to let that spoil our fun: we're away from home with seven whole days at our disposal, which will be great when it stops raining.

Our very first morning, at eight o'clock on the dot, it starts. I don't mean the rain, although it hasn't ceased all night and I can still hear it lashing against the window pane. None of the others has surfaced yet from underneath the blankets. No doubt they will at any minute now, because, disturbing our morning slumber is the incessant sound of what I assume to be a pneumatic drill coming from right under our bedroom window.

I jump out of bed and pull back the thin, faded yellow curtains. Sure enough, there they are, workmen busy all along the sea front, intent on drilling numerous holes in the road. There'll be no lie-ins on this holiday.

"I brought the tea-towels, Jill brought the toilet rolls and *you* were supposed to bring the table mats." Alison looks accusingly at me.

I shrug. "Well, I've said I'm sorry. I just forgot, or perhaps there wasn't enough room in my case. I really can't remember."

"You mean you don't care." And Alison clashes down the knives and forks. "Now what do we do?" she continues. "The landlady stated in her letter specifically what we needed to bring with us."

"Oh, stop fussing," interrupts Brenda, in her slow, easy-going way. "Here, use these magazines instead. The plates aren't that hot anyway."

Alison and I stop glaring at each other and start to laugh. I begin to set the table using Brenda's makeshift mats.

"We're really pigging it, aren't we? It's a good job my

mother isn't here. She wouldn't approve at all. Eating our dinners on *Woman's Own!*"

"This is a far cry from digs in Northgate," Alison says. "Just think, we don't need to tell Mrs P how many baths we want ever again."

"Or hide our treacle tin behind the books," smirks Jill.

"She was so prim and proper and clean, but she never really *knew* us," Alison complains. "We might have been cardboard cut-outs as far as she was concerned."

We dish out our meal of mince, sliced potatoes and tinned peas from the saucepan onto the plates and decide where to sit at the table, depending upon which magazine we fancy. This is a strange sort of setting for a kitchen-diner, with a double bed taking up half the room. I shudder to imagine how the sheets will smell of mince and onions by the end of the week. And the view out of the window still hasn't improved, as the rain continues to pour down and we can't see any further than the opposite roofs through the grey murkiness.

Once we're all settled and tucking in to our evening meal, the conversation turns to the end of the summer term last month.

"Talking about being clean and spotless," I begin. "Did I tell you about the very last day, after the rest of you had gone home?"

"No!" Alison, Jill and Brenda reply together. Everyone is eager to hear about it. "What happened?"

Now I have their attention, I put down my knife and fork. "Well, when I got back to our digs, after I'd set you off down at the bus station, I still had about half an hour to wait for Pete, my brother-in-law, to come and pick me up. I thought I'd just have one last look in our study room. I wish you'd seen the place. You would never have recognised it."

"Why, what was it like?" asks Alison.

"While we were out, Mrs P had been and transformed the whole room. You remember all the covers everywhere? There wasn't one to be seen. They'd all been removed from the sideboard and the chairs. Even the little mats had been lifted off the floor and there was a beautiful fitted carpet underneath."

There are gasps from my three erstwhile companions in digs, while Helen shakes her head.

"But that's not all," I continue. "There were vases of flowers on the sideboard and a bowl of fruit on the table."

"Sounds as if she was saying good riddance to us," says Jill, aghast.

"I felt like knocking on her kitchen door and telling her she could at least have waited until I'd gone home as well. I suppose she hadn't noticed my suitcases still standing in the hallway."

"That's the opposite of a welcome, though, isn't it?" says Jill, who is not normally the kind of person given to criticism of others. "I mean, it's usual to put flowers in a room when someone's arriving, not leaving."

"Anyway, I think I just mumbled a goodbye. I didn't even say thanks for looking after us for a year."

"Well, it's farewell Northgate and hello College for us all in September," adds Brenda in a cheery voice. "Fingers crossed we get rooms in Beechwood House, that's all I can say." She starts to collect the empty plates. "Whose turn is it for washing up? Or we could just pile them into the sink till the morning."

Helen looks horrified. "I don't blame your Mrs P for keeping her distance from you lot or covering everything up. You're so uncivilised." She moves over to the sink and pushes up her sleeves. "I'll wash. Alison, you can dry, as you brought the tea towels."

"Righto, sergeant!" Alison does a mock salute. "Just because you come from the hallowed ground of the Lake District you think we're all savages on our side of the Pennines."

We spend the week squelching rainwater in our shoes and drying off socks on all the surfaces in the flat during the evening, because we can't get the radiators to work. We splash across the Menai Bridge to spend ten minutes in Anglesey, just to say we'd set foot there. Then we turn round and splash our way back.

One day, we take shelter in a tourist attraction with a plaque outside saying 'The Smallest House in Britain' and then lie in bed that same night in fits of laughter imagining anyone who lived there would have their feet downstairs and their head upstairs.

We parade our way along the windy seafront in Llandudno and climb muddily the first few hundred yards of Snowdon before turning back. We bitterly regret having not taken the dry route to the summit instead, otherwise known as the mountain railway. As someone pointed out with wisdom, probably Helen, even if we had taken the easy way up, we would still have been robbed of the view, because of the dense fog around the peak.

It's Friday, almost the end of our holiday, and we are so sick of the Welsh rain that we go to the pictures to see 'Song of Norway'. The lady in the ticket office thinks I am half-price and the others are adults.

"You shouldn't have put your plaits in," says Alison.

"Jill's got hers in," I object.

"But she's at least six inches taller than you."

Then twenty minutes into the film, we produce our packed lunch of crab paste sandwiches. It causes some disruption when we open up crinkly paper packets and whisper to each other about passing them along.

"Pooh! Can't half smell the sea in here," pipes an irritating small boy in the row behind us. He's spent the first few minutes of the film kicking the back of Jill's seat and ignoring her glaring looks. We are forced to make a quick exit, slinking out of our seats and groping our way up the darkened aisle in uncontrollable fits of laughter. Once out into the half-light of a dismal afternoon, we agree that the film wasn't up to much anyway and not worth staying till the end. We have seen plenty of mountains here in Wales.

On our very last damp evening, we decide to eye up the local talent at the corner pub. The landlord, a burly, oversized man with a threatening Welsh lilt in his voice, refuses to serve us, as he is convinced that we are under age. Nothing can persuade him of the truth, that we are all a mature twenty years of age. When Brenda produces her students' union card showing her date of birth, he is still having none of it and firmly shows us the door, telling us we don't look a day over sixteen.

"I haven't got my plaits in this time, but I still look too young," I retort, as we trudge down the street away from the pub in a gloomy group.

"You still haven't grown though," says Alison, with a wink.

The train taking us out of Wales is a slow, jerky thing, stopping at every station. All is quiet among us. The holiday is at an end and the jollying will have to wait until we meet up again. We lean wearily back in our seats as the passing hills become rolling countryside and then a city landscape.

There's a scramble for the cases and bags when we finally reach Leeds, where we must change platforms. The crowd surges us along and before I know it, we are at the point where our paths diverge. We shout our farewells across the noisy station: "Don't forget to ring" and "See you in the third year". Even waving is out of the question as our hands are full of luggage.

I'm going home with a few photographs in the camera, but more memories stored up than could be displayed in one album. Wet Wales will live on far longer than a week of fumbling French with a stranger in a foreign country. At least, this is how I console myself.

Travelling to the Continent can wait.

CHAPTER THIRTY-ONE

~~~

SEPTEMBER 1971

A ROOM OF MY OWN

It's always sunny at Bishopsfield. At least it seems to be.

It's sunny on the first day of our last year. I'm trying not to think of it like that – the last year. Otherwise, everything will be the last. The last Christmas, the last Easter, the last summer term. No, I'll think of it just as arriving once again. It's back to greenery and trees and autumn leaves and switching from my home world of family to my new world of friends. It's an easy change now. I've grown into it.

Mam and I, laden down with an assortment of bags and Pete bringing up the rear, follow the path across the grass. We're heading for Beechwood House, St Mag's newly built Hall of Residence, to begin my third and final year.

Oh dear. I wasn't going to use that word – final.

A room of my own, complete with washbasin, awaits me. When the letter arrived from College during the summer holidays to inform me that my first choice of Hall of Residence was successful, I was overjoyed. I explain to Mam how *modern* it is: all single rooms, complete with our own washbasins, no more sharing and more importantly, no landladies and no tiptoeing to the bathroom to keep a caretaker happy.

"This is your room!" yell Alison and Jill across the lawns, hanging out of a ground floor window.

Mam looks at me with disbelief on her face. "How can that be *your* room, when *they're* already in it?"

It feels so good to be back, with everyone in everyone else's rooms and calling out comments to each other. This is something my mother doesn't understand, as she has never experienced communal living, nor does she ever want to, as she once told me.

I have to admit I feel relieved when Mam decides after only about twenty minutes that it's time to head for home. The commotion that goes with being in the midst of excited twenty-year-olds behaving like twelve-year-olds doesn't suit her. As I wave a cheery goodbye to her and Pete, my overriding thought is: how quickly can I get back into the mayhem and get settled in?

"I'm never going to get sorted in here if you two don't get out," I pretend to complain in mock tones to Alison and Jill. Although they have rooms of their own next door to mine on the ground floor, they are both in here, investigating my cupboards and drawers.

"Have you seen your sink?" asks Alison, opening the two middle wooden doors of what I assume is the wardrobe. Instead they reveal a cream-coloured washbasin, which I think might be described as a vanity unit, with the added luxury of a mirror. This is going to be my pride and joy while living here in Beechwood House.

"I forgot we have sinks of our own," I lie, trying not to show my enthusiasm. But I can't help myself. "This is marvellous!" And I start to arrange the contents of my toilet bag around the edge of the sink, including my pink Avon soap-on-a-rope. I try closing the double doors and then opening them again, to get the full effect of the soapy perfume.

"And just look at the view," muses Jill. She kneels up on the bed and gazes out of the large picture window.

"Why, what's good about it?" I ask. I'm too busy trying to organise everything, clambering up on a chair to reach the top cupboards. "Hand me those things, will you, Alison?"

"You can see across to the White Gates," Jill informs us. "So you'll notice if anyone's climbing over them after dark. Then they can come and knock on the window and you can let them in, being as you're right next to the front door."

I turn and look at her from my lofty height. "I don't

know what's good about that. Sounds like a big drawback to being in Room 1, if you ask me."

"Plus, there's a full view of chapel," Jill continues brightly.

Our chapel at St Mag's is an ultra-modern affair, with lots of glass down to the floor and a roof made up of several flat parts at different angles: a bit like a tent pitched in the desert. It certainly isn't boxy or boring, words which could be used to describe many other buildings built in the 1960s. I suppose Beechwood House, being very new, might fall into that category: essentially, it's two boxes joined together in an L-shape, with rows of square windows on three floors.

"I might go to chapel one Sunday, now we're so handy," I announce.

"You're not going to become one of the 'God squad', are you?" asks Alison. "You know, the ones who walk around with Bibles?"

I smile. "No, I'm not that religious. I might join the chapel orchestra though, now I've reached Lesson 10 in my 'Learn to play the Recorder' book. Very useful for Teaching Practice."

I begin opening drawers at random, not knowing where to start. I choose the deepest one and throw in a few jumpers from my suitcase.

"How am I going to manage without you Jill? I'll have no one to sort me out."

"Don't worry dear. I'm just next door in Room 2 and

Alison is number 3. We have no view at all looking out at the back. Oh, and Brenda's number 4. She's just gone to find out if there's a coach going to Leeds tomorrow night for the dance."

Alison begins to rearrange my piles of books and files on the top of my desk. "Did you realise we've got study lamps?"

"Switch it on and let's see what it's like. Makes you actually want to work, doesn't it?" I feel overjoyed with everything. "What about the common room? Where is it? I wonder if it has a telly, and more to the point…"

"Does it work?" Alison and I chorus together.

"Don't know," Jill says, bouncing herself off my bed. "Give us a chance to finish putting our stuff away and we'll have a wander and find out."

As the two of them leave me to my unpacking, Alison sticks her head around the door and adds as a parting shot, "And we've got two bathrooms on our corridor!"

I answer back, "Bagsy the nearest one after high tea tonight!"

We sit in the midst of a mountain of food: plates of chips and fried eggs, several apples, bananas, piles of cream crackers, hunks of cheese and mounds of white, sliced bread. The aroma is so tempting it is little wonder that high tea is one of our weekly highlights.

"Catherine, what are you doing?" Alison shakes her head at the girl sitting opposite, who happens to come from my part of the country. We have sometimes kept each other company on the express bus home when Judith and Pete can't pick me up.

"I'm just mashing up my banana," Catherine answers calmly.

"Yes, but pouring milk over it as well?" says Alison. "I don't know how you can actually eat that."

Meanwhile, I am ladling strawberry jam onto a slice of bread. "Well, I'm going to have cheese on this," I say, to level up the situation.

"Never heard of cheese and jam together," butts in Brenda.

"And there's me thinking it's a proper Yorkshire thing."

"It's cheese and apple pie. Or cheese and fruit cake," says Alison.

It's no good, I tell myself, the Yorkshire folk will never agree with Catherine and me.

Alison tells us to hurry up eating our strange concoctions, and suggests we collect up some of the left overs to take back for supper. So, we bundle out of the dining hall, add our empty plates to the already tottering tower on the trolley and stagger out balancing piles of bread, packets of cream crackers and apples.

"Anyone got any butter?" Brenda yells up the corridor as we walk into Beechwood.

"Helen's quite likely to have some," says Alison. "She's coming over tonight. I'll give her a ring on the internal phone."

My room is packed full of people. Everyone, including Catherine, drapes themselves over the bed, the chair and the floor, with Helen expected to add to the crowd later. My desk is covered with our purloined items from the dining hall to feast upon for supper. So much for having a room of my own to study in peace and quiet, I think. But tonight, work can wait.

Meanwhile we make plans to have toast while we watch the late-night film in the common room. That is, if we can get the dodgy television to work.

CHAPTER THIRTY-TWO

~~~~~

AN EMERGENCY
AT THE PICTURES

Crouching for half an hour behind a Wendy House in the corner of a busy nursery class with an ear right up to its gingham curtains is not to be recommended. That is, if you don't want rigor mortis to set in. Trying to operate a reel-to-reel tape recorder without some three-year-old child falling over your legs and asking what you are doing makes the situation even worse. On top of all of this, being forced to listen to every word uttered by these little people, all fully immersed in imaginary play, renders the experience quite surreal.

Unless you happen to have a Special Study to write.

At St Mag's, this is the official title of an extremely long essay or a very slim book. And the fact that I'm hiding in some dark corner of a nursery classroom is all my own doing, as I've chosen 'The Development of Language in the Pre-school Child' as my title. So far, I've covered the incoherent babblings of a baby in a high chair, writing down its every ooh and aah. I've sat on park benches observing curly-headed tots being pushed on swings and shouting out commands to mothers, 'Again, again!' It's a wonder I didn't attract more attention and get arrested.

Every word uttered at the scene must be noted and analysed later back at Beechwood House, in the confines of my wonderful room with a view and a washbasin. Yes, I still regard it as living in luxury, especially every time I open those cupboard doors and bathe in the sweet aroma of my pink soap-on-a-rope. I can conjure up that smell any time I wish.

My self-imposed question staring out from the blank page in front of me asks, 'Do children make up their own grammar rules?' One little boy called Kevin explained to me, 'I comed to school this morning with my mummy'. If it's 'walked' and 'talked' then he assumes it must be 'comed'. And at what age do they apply the correct past tense? Fascinating.

And then there are those who still have not mastered which pronoun to use. 'Me show you'. Should you correct them, or will they discover this for themselves? Intriguing.

My morning spent behind the Wendy House has resulted in my recording a one-way conversation involving a little girl with enormous ribbons in her hair who is trying to boss about a quiet boy who spoke hardly a word. He was not the most useful example to study. She told him to 'get on with the washing up' after she had tipped a vast array of garishly coloured plastic dishes into the miniature sink. He dumbly refused to do so by spending the next ten minutes trying to crawl inside the equally miniature cupboard underneath. At this point, the beribboned little girl became bored and wandered away towards the sand tray.

Which of the actions played out in the Wendy House are imitations of real life, I wonder, and which spring entirely from the child's imagination?

Observing and making sense of all this language, or lack of it, might be regarded by some as a tedious task, but I find myself engrossed in the subject. It involves careful listening and lots of scribbling and poring over piles of text books before you bash out endless pages of typing. One mistake and out must come the correction fluid, producing white blobs here and there. The hours fly by unnoticed.

We find having a room of one's own is essential. It's fine to have company, but when a deadline is looming ever nearer, we all retire to our hideaways and work until long after the autumn sky darkens.

It's October and it's mutually agreed that we need a well-earned break. Alison and Jill are determined they want to go to the pictures, whichever film is showing. I complain that anything that has Dracula as its central character will be far too horrific and the last thing I want to do is to contaminate my mind with such rubbish, etcetera, etcetera. The pair of them say that even watching a horror film is better than another night of work, work, work.

Friday night, early, Alison and Jill duly set off in plenty of time to grab a good seat for a night of fright. Brenda and I ask Catherine and Helen over to Beechwood for a nice lazy evening, doing nothing much. Catherine hardly needs inviting. She's a daily visitor.

"I hope you haven't brought your usual carrier bag, mind," I joke, as she slings her anorak over the back of my chair.

"Why? What's usually in it?" asks Helen. She stretches out on my bed with some knitting and tucks her feet under my red tartan rug.

"Oh, just my washing. No, I haven't got it. I'm bringing it over tomorrow. You really don't mind me leaving it here, do you?"

I shake my head and smile. "Of course not. Feel free to make yourself at home."

"Usually after lectures, I use Beechwood's spin dryer," Catherine explains to Helen in a matter-of-fact way.

She looks up from her knitting. "What's your college flat like?"

"Not as nice as Beechwood. There's no spin dryer, for a start. The funny thing is, Miss Hindmarch thinks I live here. I went to her room down the end of the first year's corridor last week for my history tutorial and I forgot I still had my slippers on. Then daft Miss Hindmarch put a note for me in the pigeonholes."

Helen thinks it's no wonder, when Catherine is wandering round in her slippers and with carrier bags full of washing. She resumes her knitting, which she explains will eventually turn into a pull-on hat for the winter, and we all marvel at her complicated pattern.

Seated at my desk, Catherine spreads out some last-minute notes to copy up and Brenda arrives armed with mugs of coffee and a full packet of digestives to share.

Twenty minutes later, when we have demolished the last biscuit, Helen shoves the unfinished hat into her knitting bag and declares she is famished. "Have you got anything else to eat?"

I root around in the cupboards, but there's no sign of so much as a cream cracker, or even one left-over stale slice of bread.

"Anyone fancy going down for fish and chips?" asks Catherine.

I pull back the curtains, only to see blackness and a rain-spotted window. "Not in this weather. We should have told Alison and Jill to bring some on their way up from town."

"We weren't hungry then. Pity we couldn't send them a message," says Helen.

Silence fills the room while we look around at each

other, aware of our now desperate hunger pangs. Then someone says, "Let's ring up the pictures and ask them to bring up four lots of fish and chips."

The idea hangs in the air like a temptation that seems too daring to try.

In the confines of the trunk room, all four of us huddle round the phone. Catherine, our courageous spokeswoman, performs the deed of dialling the number of the Odeon, ready to speak in a put-on posh voice.

Helen and I exchange guilty glances. Is this exciting, scary or just downright wrong? I can't decide.

"Can I speak to the manager?" Muffled giggles and a stern shush from Catherine. "I need to speak to my two friends who are in the audience tonight. It's an emergency."

An hour and a half later, as we stuff ourselves with illicit fat chips, Jill regales her side of the story with a great deal of glee. She describes how she was shaking with trepidation as the manager handed her the phone in his office and then continued to hover in the background.

"When the usherette came down the aisle with her torch and told us there was an emergency call for us, I thought someone had died!"

"And then," continues Alison, "when Jill yelled into the receiver, 'How many lots?' I told her to try and look devastated, as if a loved one had left this earth."

"I didn't need to try to look devastated – I was!" retorts Jill.

It's hard to laugh when your mouth is full of fish and chips.

After our two friends act out the drama of the fake emergency, they point out that they were the innocent victims and had not expected a real night of fright. The rest of us are forced to promise that we will never, under any circumstances, even under intense hunger, try the same trick again.

~~~

CHAPTER THIRTY-THREE

A BUNCH OF
DEAD FLOWERS

It's our Wednesday afternoon Drama session, where we expect some light relief from heavy lectures and writing long essays. Miss Featheringale is young, slim and attractive: attributes not found in great abundance in lecturers at St Mag's. She doesn't just walk in the ordinary sense of the word: she slops along. Her shoes look as if they don't quite fit properly as her slingbacks flap along with her. The sound of her slip-slop kitten heels heralds her arrival as we wait in the hall, sitting cross-legged on the floor in our groups. She's wearing a tight-fitting blouse, dangerously unbuttoned down to her cleavage and carelessly tucked into a mini-skirt. Definitely not our average type of lecturer, but she fits the picture of a laid-back Drama teacher to perfection.

Preferring to shun the limelight, my mouth feels dry wondering what challenge awaits us in this week's topic. I wish I'd had time to finish my morning mug of coffee.

With no notes in front of her, Miss Featheringale gazes around at us all and announces in a quiet, mysterious way in her seductive, husky voice, "Today, ladies and gentlemen…"

The male students, about half a dozen of them in all, sit up straighter, wide-eyed, no doubt admiring her careless attire.

"Today, I want you to produce a kaleidoscope of words and feelings."

Alison and I exchange nervous glances. What can that mean?

"You can use poetry, prose and…" – she pauses for effect – "music."

I feel only slightly better.

Moving, or rather slopping, from group to group, our modern, innovative Drama lecturer hands out folded pieces of paper, telling us a different topic title is printed on each one. On opening ours, staring out at us, handwritten in block capitals, is one word: 'WAR'. I feel defeated by the subject before we even start. How do we make a kaleidoscope of war? Seconds tick by and no one moves or says a word.

Miss Featheringale claps her hands to galvanise us into action. "I'll give you an hour to go off, sort something out and then be back here at half past two to perform."

We never give a second's thought to the activities of these so-called hard-working lecturers during our 'going off' time. What are they doing while they have no students in front of them? Once, in a Maths lecture during the first year, our group was told to 'go off with the surveying equipment' and return with answers to various impossible problems. Such as: find the angle from a certain point on the ground to the apex of the chapel roof. And other boring, insurmountable riddles.

Of course, someone else did the surveying and my contribution to our group's efforts was to provide mugs of coffee all round. A fat lot of surveying I learnt, but then I can't imagine the lack of it hindering my progress in life. If I want any surveying doing, then surely the common sense approach would be to contact a surveyor. It's being a teacher of young children which I am aiming for.

Now that we have been handed the great subject of War, I remind myself that it's words and music which are more in my line of expertise, unlike problems in Maths. Miss Featheringale has challenged us and, as a main English student, I tell myself that I am ready and eager to 'go off' and help to produce some weird and wonderful kaleidoscope. I feel tremendously cheered up.

"Come on, my room," orders one of the girls in our

'War' group. "Mine's the nearest. Coffee first. Then discussion."

This goes without saying. Digestive biscuits and powdered milk make their familiar appearance as soon as eight of us have squeezed into the room. We spill over the one single bed, the one armchair and the one study chair behind the desk. Our collective array of books is formidable. There's a pile in the middle of the floor consisting of a whole range of poetry books which we've been instructed to bring along.

Now that hot, steaming coffee and tea in mugs are handed out, someone begins, straight to the point. "War. Which war do you reckon?"

"The most romantic."

"I don't think there is such a thing as a romantic war."

To make it more specific, I offer a suggestion. "The one which produced the most romantic poetry was the First World War."

Alison, sitting cross-legged in this crowded study room, helps me out. "That's right. There's Rupert Brooke, Siegfried Sassoon, Wilfred Owen, plenty to choose from. Bet we'll get funds of examples we can work with."

I can feel the excitement building as we thumb through pages and pages of verse, scribbling down descriptive passages. The poem which catches our imagination the most is Wilfred Owen's 'Dulce et Decorum Est', with its first lines:

Bent double, like old beggars under sacks,
Knock-kneed, coughing like hags, we cursed
through sludge.

We can see the possibilities here to act it out. Then an idea comes up which is an inspirational one. A girl who'd been quiet up to now says, "I've got a Simon and Garfunkel record and the last track is 'Silent Night'.

"What's that got to do with war?" remarks the owner of the room, with a slight hint of sarcasm.

"Because over the top of the song," the quiet girl explains, "you hear a newsreader listing the names of soldiers killed during the Vietnam war."

It's unanimously agreed that this would be the ideal way to finish our drama. But how to start it?

Alison sits up after scanning the poetry books and points a finger in the air.

"How about 'Revolution' by the Beatles? The words are just right, about how we're going to have a revolution and change the world."

I glance round. All faces are receptive, interested, lights dancing in our eyes: this has really gripped us.

Again, the room owner speaks up, assuming a kind of leadership. "Right. So, we start with 'Revolution'. Who's got that, by the way?"

Alison jumps to her feet. "Brenda, over in Beechwood. If she's not in, I know she won't mind if I just borrow it." And the next second, she is out of the door.

The girl with the Simon and Garfunkel record suggests that for the first line of the poem, 'Bent double, like old beggars', some of us could be soldiers, marching in while 'Revolution' is playing.

"Great idea," we all chorus.

Our assumed leader waves her hands. "What could we use for guns?"

"Umbrellas?"

"Nobody's got any."

"Hockey sticks. We can get those from the games cupboard in the PE department."

"Right. Come marching across the stage with hockey sticks. Background music, 'Revolution'. Then what?"

"Well, if we're supposed to end up dead, ready for 'Silent Night', we'd better have a battle."

"Got a better idea. Why not drop dead from imaginary bullets?"

"Yes, as if they're coming from the audience. That would work."

And the ideas are scribbled down onto a sheet of paper.

At this point, Alison stumbles in through the door, steps over several pairs of legs and puts the borrowed LP on the desk. "It's a double album and 'Revolution' is on the second LP, side four. How much longer have we got before we have to report back?" she asks, urgently.

"About ten minutes. So far, everyone's lying dead and listening to Simon and Garfunkel's 'Silent Night'. We need something else."

I leap up, as if I've been hit in the back. "Flowers!" I shout. "One of us could strew flowers over the dead soldiers."

Alison was at the ready once more. "I'll pop up the corridor and see if anyone's got any." Before she disappears again, she adds, "If we're lucky."

During the next two minutes, somehow I am elected to be the narrator and also the person to scatter the flowers at the end.

Alison reappears. I look up and see her standing in the doorway, her hands behind her.

"The good news is, I've got a few carnations." She produces from behind her back a bunch of wilted flowers, the once-red colour of their petals turning to brown around the edges and their leaves drooping and curled.

"The bad news is, they're dead."

Our faces fall. We've run out of time: the hour is up.

Record player at the ready, our self-appointed leader is positioned to manipulate the volume knob and change LPs. I perch on the edge of the stage, poems in hand. I'm relieved no acting is required, only reading. And I can handle that. In the middle of the watching groups of students, Miss Featheringale sits upright on a hard, plastic chair, eager to see what her protégés can produce.

The Beatles begin with their 'Revolution' and the student soldiers march across the stage, hockey sticks resting on their shoulders like rifles. The volume of the music gradually lowers. I begin with the lines of poetry we have chosen, giving it all the drama I can.

> *Bent double, like old beggars under sacks,*
> *Knock kneed, coughing like hags, we cursed*
> *through sludge.*

The soldiers become like old men staggering along with walking sticks. Using no sound effects, an imaginary volley of shots causes the student actors to turn towards the audience, clutching at their chests before slumping slowly one by one to the floor. 'Silent Night' opens with the gentle voices of Simon and Garfunkel, while in the background, names of victims of war are read out in monotones: quietly at first, gradually becoming louder, until the music is overtaken and all that can be heard is name after name of the dead.

I walk across the stage and carefully place on the back of each 'fallen soldier' a withered, dead carnation. We had no choice. They were all we had.

There is one, long, magnificent hush. Miss Featheringale stands up, pushes back her chair and begins to clap. Soon everyone is joining in the applause.

I feel a sense of pride welling up. The faces of the others glow similarly pink. We have done well, after all. The ending wasn't spoilt.

"To turn the guns into walking sticks, that was brilliant. But the flowers ..."

She holds her arms outstretched towards us. Floppy Featheringale isn't a Drama lecturer for nothing.

Her voice rises another octave and quivers, "The dropping of a single dead flower on each body was... superb."

She turns towards the rest of the students: they who are now insignificant, they who have given only second-rate productions.

"Not a live flower, but a *dead* flower. What inspiration!"

Now we look at one another, keeping our pride suppressed. None of us dare breathe or mention that although we had thought of the flowers, it was pure chance that someone had forgotten to put water in the vase.

CHAPTER THIRTY-FOUR

~~~~~

THE PACE QUICKENS

Oh, the glory of waking up on a Saturday morning, knowing there's no hurry to get up. I push to one side that essay, promising I'll tackle it later, and shout to ask Jill if she's going down town.

We amble across the College path, disturb the piles of leaves the gardeners have so carefully swept up and pick a few of the brightest ones to press later under the *Oxford Illustrated Dictionary*. The pace is slow, the conversation animated and our worries limited to what concoctions will be on offer at high tea.

Mondays to Fridays are different. The alarm clocks puncture our slumber while it's still dark, and after coffee and a digestive biscuit we dash off to the Lecture Block with the relevant file. With varying attention, depending on which lecturer is in full flow, we scribble down notes and make fun of the catch phrases we hear, like Mr Taylor, who at every opportunity reminds us to 'Keep your files ticking over, ladies'.

Sometimes it's a double session of Art, when we are sent off to find and draw a knot in the floorboards of the corridor, or paint from real life a cage of bantam hens, or try tie-dye, or my least favourite, struggle to knock nails into a wooden frame to make a weaving loom. I'm lucky that Catherine comes to my rescue.

Just as I'm thinking the timetable is finished for the day, I remember chapel orchestra practice. I dive back to my room, collect my precious wooden recorder and hare over to chapel, where I take my place in the back row. I have become quite adept at miming the high, unattainable notes by moving my fingers over the correct holes but refraining to blow. I tell myself, it's all good experience.

But, as the autumn term progresses, there is one huge worry looming. Final Teaching Practice. Dreaded by all.

Any day now, the lists will be pinned up on the main notice board, informing us of our places in schools for eleven weeks, starting as soon as we come back after the New Year. Eleven weeks! Almost a whole term.

In our gloomy moments, we often wonder why we have decided to teach when everyone dreads the onslaught of Teaching Practice so much. We keep telling ourselves that it will all be so different once we are out in the real world with classes of our own. Will we still feel that churning stomach every Sunday evening then, with the thoughts of having to perform in front of thirty little bodies the next morning?

Now, it's after the autumn half term and just as predicted, the list is up. There's a permanent crowd around it, so I persuade Jill to squirm through for me and report back. She emerges bright and smiling.

"I'm at Harrogate, which is not too bad, quite a good area actually. Guess where you are."

"No idea. Go on, put me out of my misery," I plead, clenching my hands together.

"Bishopsfield."

"Here? I can't be."

"You certainly are. You're at St Paul's RC School on the opposite side of the road to Cottages."

We jump up and down together in delight.

"I can't believe my luck. That means, I won't have to go on the college bus. I can just walk along."

"I know, you jammy thing. Alison and I are going to have to get up at six o'clock every morning."

November, and it's Jill's birthday. The start of all our special birthdays, when we reach the age of twenty-one and the state of adulthood, although legally we attained that status back in 1970. St Mag's has at last caught up and we now possess keys to our rooms, although no one makes regular use of them. We remain free and easy.

So far our slim grants, with some much slimmer than others, have meant scrounging the market for presents for the family, with none at all for each other at College. But this year it's different. We're clubbing together and combining money and ideas.

Not content with the little shops in Bishopsfield, Helen, Alison and I head off on the bus to Harrogate with its vast choice of establishments, while Jill is safely spending some time with her parents at home. We finally discover a keepsake ornament, which looks as if it were made for her. In the window of a gift shop we spy, at a bargain price, a dear little pottery bunny with lop-sided ears, propping up a hollow tree trunk: ideal to hold a miniature bunch of wild flowers. That is, if she cuts off most of their stalks.

Together with an illustrated book about animals, this present seems to fit Jill perfectly and we leave the shop with the precious purchase, feeling very pleased with ourselves.

No one can visit this spa town without eyeing up the fashions on display, and I fancy myself in a huge navy blue cape with a red lining. But as always, the price tag proves too forbidding, and I make a private plan to ask Judith to get out her old sewing machine instead.

To complete the perfect shopping day, the three of us treat ourselves to a cream scone in the most prestigious tea shop, where the waitresses all wear white frilly-edged aprons over black dresses. Helen is in her element in these surroundings, and she joins in the giggles while we drink our frothy coffee and lick cream off our chins.

With almost empty purses, we gather up our shopping bags, leave the warmth and the chatter of the café behind and step out into the nip of the late autumn air. There's just time to catch the four o'clock bus back to College, where, if we're lucky, we might make it to the dining hall before they begin serving high tea.

It's December and the holly and the ivy hang like a bower, making an arch in the middle of the corridor. Disney characters adorn the walls and home-made streamers are strung criss-cross from outside my door right up to the common room at the other end.

We're having a five-minute breather before embarking upon lectures on the last timetabled day of term. Tomorrow, it's home for Christmas. Essays and that dreaded file about the teaching of reading that we've been reminded now for weeks to 'keep ticking over' have to be handed in, the cause of many a late night this week.

My door stands open so that we can all sit and gaze upon our creative activities, the tinsel glistening and glimmering in the lights all the way up the corridor.

"Do you think we've got any chance of winning?" asks Alison.

"Not a hope," says Jill, ever realistic. "Have you seen the decorations in the third-year middle block? They've done Cinderella and it's fabulous. A huge painted coach and horses and everything."

Brenda shrugs and reaches for the digestives on my desk.

"Well it would be. Some of them are main Art up that corridor. What's the prize anyway?"

"Tea with Her Majesty the Principal, I expect," I giggle.

"Lord, I hope we don't win then," Alison says, before indulging in a huge loud yawn. "I can't believe we've been up for three hours already and it's still not light yet. You really missed a treat, Brenda, slumbering in bed like that. You won't have another opportunity, you know."

"Do you mean I won't get the chance to stand around outside in the cold and dark at six o'clock in the morning? Boo hoo. What a shame."

"Well I admit it was rather freezing. But worth it. You do realise Brenda, that's the last time we shall ever carol sing to the first years?" I sob, mockingly.

"You promised not to mention 'last times', remember?" Alison reminds me.

"I'll never forget though, when we were in Dale House. Do you remember, Jill, the sound of the singing coming along the corridor?"

"That's something I could never forget." She jumps off my bed and starts gathering up the coffee mugs. "Talking about singing, what time's the carol service this afternoon?"

I scrabble among the jumble of papers strewn across the desk until I find a list written on a notepad. "Half past two. Which reminds me, I'm supposed to be at choir practice straight after lectures at twelve, which means going into second dinners. Hope there'll still be some choices left. I hate turkey and the reek of soggy sprouts."

Jill dumps the mugs in my sink, straightens her long dark plaits and picks up her pile of files from the floor. "Well, we're off to History. We'll say 'Happy Christmas' to Catherine for you. See you after lectures."

Brenda leaps to her feet now. "It's in the Lecture Block. We'll have to run."

And they both disappear.

Alison and I gather our things together in a more leisurely fashion and we leave without bothering to lock our rooms. The front door of Beechwood House swings shut behind us as we step out into the sharp December air. The sky is just beginning to lighten to a gloomy grey and the paths between the dark lawns still look dangerously frosty.

"Mr Bainbridge once said in a lecture that he enjoys every day of his life," Alison muses.

"I know. When he wakes up, he says today is the beginning of the rest of his life. Do you think he knows that we hang onto his every word?"

We pass the chapel and head towards College for our tutorial.

"Main English, here we come. Mr Bainbridge, we love you."

~~~

CHAPTER THIRTY-FIVE

JANUARY TO MARCH 1972

A COUNTRY COTTAGE DELIGHT

The long white-painted cottage glistens in the cold January sunshine, with its small square windows and low, front door looking out onto, surprisingly, a miniature playground surrounded by a high railing. This is no country residence but a classroom in a cottage. Here I am to spend eleven weeks on final Teaching Practice, long, hard-working weeks. For my daily commute, I have only to walk along College Road, fringed by tall waving trees. I shall watch winter turn into spring.

The rest of the school buildings, looking far more conventional, brick built with high Victorian windows, are across the road, opposite the white cottage. My classroom happens to be an overspill for the youngest children, a homely, cosy place for education, made up of three square rooms with their connecting doors removed. The first room houses a piano and the library books, the second, where more formal teaching is done, is furnished with wooden desks and a blackboard, and the third serves as the messy area with painting easels, sand and water. There is no room for a weary teacher to sit down. I must huddle inside a large cupboard to make cups of coffee at playtime, along with my class teacher, lovely, friendly Mrs Bell, before heading straight out into the yard. No skulking away in a staff room to enjoy any peace and quiet, or to join in the chatter of the other teachers.

No. We are 'on duty' morning and afternoon. It feels as if I am in a remote one-class school in the middle of the country.

This being a Roman Catholic school, the children come from not only Bishopsfield itself but also the surrounding area, from farms and villages up into the dale. As January marches into February, I am handed tiny bunches of snowdrops, picked while my pupils wait, wrapped up against the chill winds, for taxis to collect them. We sing Peter Rabbit songs while I accompany them on the piano, write stories at the desks, paint big pictures in the messy room and go for walks along the river, down what is locally named the 'Fairy Steps'. We present an assembly in the big school hall, my class warbling, '*I love the sun, it shines on me, God made the sun and God made me*', while I strum three chords on the guitar, without pauses between changes. The Roman Catholic staff, unused to hearing such songs, adore its simple message.

With a class of around twenty children, this is how I imagine teaching to be: Timothy regaling me with long accounts of the CS Lewis books he is reading at home with his mother, Jeremy with his endearing lisp and little Claire with two bunches in her hair which bob as she talks. They don't run round the yard wildly, or shuffle during story-time or daub paint on their faces: they are good but not angelic, delightful but not entirely innocent.

Oh, that the poor, deprived town children could be transported to a country delight where there is a bird table outside the window, where they can watch trees change through the seasons and have a view of the high, wide sky. It is no small wonder that children mostly paint a narrow, blue strip at the top of their paper, as those who live among streets of houses only ever see sky above the chimney pots: it never seems to reach the ground. They can't feel the heaviness of big, frothy clouds or notice the snow heading towards them in a grey mist.

Living on the coast, as a child I was always aware that the sky touched the sea along the line of the horizon, with a difference in their shades of blue. An old teacher of mine in the first year at junior school used to repeat the mantra in our weekly Art lesson, 'Blue and green should never be seen', an adage I refused to believe in. At the age of seven, I thought, well, what about the blue of the sea and the green grass on the cliff tops?

I know that I am happy here, in my country-style classroom. And when I feel happy, I feel confident. When my tutor comes in to observe me, she remarks that it seems I have been teaching there all year.

One afternoon, while Mrs Bell is at a meeting, I experience the luxury of having the sole supervision of the children, the classrooms and the little yard. The headmistress chooses a reliable top junior girl to stay with us, just in case I need to send a message across to the main school in an emergency. There is no telephone. For a few hours I have become Miss Hardy, a teacher in charge of an infant class. Is it preparation for the moment when I am faced with my own set of children, come September, once College is left behind? I am not so sure. Here, I am practising and perfecting my teaching skills, but as my sister keeps reminding me, it takes years and experience to create a good teacher.

There's still a long way to go.

CHAPTER THIRTY-SIX

~~~

AN INNOCENT
IN THE CAPITAL

"Do you fancy a trip to London?" Helen asks me on our way out of an English lecture.

I can hardly concentrate on the question. Mr Bainbridge has been extolling the wonders of the love poetry of John Donne, convincing us that somewhere out there is another soul destined to meet ours and I am still captivated: '*My face in thine eye, thine in mine appears.*'

Our esteemed lecturer tells us a story of how, before his second child was born, he did not know how his love could expand to encompass another, and yet it did. Therefore, love has no bounds. Once again, as in all of his lectures, we are enraptured by his words. And yet, we say nothing. We listen and write and hand in essays and I vow, one day, sometime in the future, I will tell him how much we hang on to his every word.

Eventually, I am brought back to reality.

London? The total sum of my experience of our capital is a visit lasting a couple of hours with Fran, my room-mate from the first year. I remember we had a very expensive coffee in a crowded café and then mingled with the crowds and dodged the pigeons in Trafalgar Square. It only served to whet my appetite. There is far more to see: The Houses of Parliament, the boats on the river Thames, the grand shops on Oxford Street. I could get excited.

"If I had a chance, yes, I'd like to go to London. Who's going?"

Helen falls in step with Alison and me around the Mature Students' Hut and across the Lecture Block path.

"There's a list gone up on the main notice board for a day trip on the first weekend in June. Fancy it?"

"A *day* trip? From here? How can we manage that?"

At the long boards which stretch the length of the corridor in main College, Helen reads out the notice: "'Leaving Bishopsfield at 3am, arriving in London in time for breakfast. Free day. Coach leaves London at 11.30pm.' So, are you two putting your names down?"

"I definitely will," Alison says immediately.

"That's no sleep for two nights," I groan.

But Helen sounds keen to go. "Well, you could go to bed early and get up for three."

"I suppose so. Go on then. I will, if you two are,"

I grunt. "What about Jill? Put her name down as well. We'll break the news gently."

There are six of us altogether: Helen, Brenda, Alison, Jill, who has had no choice in the matter, and Catherine, being the most familiar with the capital, to ensure we don't get lost on the underground. And me, the small-town girl who still can't find her way around Newcastle.

We have good intentions of going to bed tonight nice and early, until someone looks in the paper and discovers there's a Marx Brothers film on at midnight, so, we end up gathering in the common room in Beechwood House, ready with packets of crisps and chocolate biscuits to watch 'Duck Soup'. Then Alison spends a good part of an hour wandering around with the aerial, climbing on the furniture trying to get a picture that isn't distorted.

By one o'clock, Groucho has us in hysterics and we're still laughing by the time we get on the coach at three. But when we stop at a motorway services for breakfast at six in the morning, we feel quite ill. It keeps coming over us in waves all day. For a little while, we revert to normal and then, one of us collapses in a heap wherever we happen to be and the rest of us have to stop and wait until the feeling passes. We spend at least twenty minutes sitting on the steps of Marks and Spencer's, waiting for Jill to recover. That's Alison's choice: the biggest Marks and Spencer's in the world. We have each chosen one venue for the day and by some miracle, I believe we will manage every one of them. With careful planning of course.

I choose a boat ride up the River Thames. From there, we walk to the Victoria and Albert Museum, Helen's choice. Catherine leads the way. The city is like a maze to me. I feel like a country bumpkin. Jill is used to the metropolitan city of Bradford and Catherine is used to dodging across Newcastle: pressing the button for the little green man is second nature to her. I was brought up in a small cul-de-sac of a town by the sea, where there is only a zebra crossing to manage to get to the one street of shops.

"Where're we going now?" I ask Jill, as I quicken my steps to keep up with our punishing schedule.

"Biba's, I think. Catherine's choice."

"What on earth is that?" I shriek. "Never heard of it."

Catherine turns round. "It's the best boutique going at the moment. Got all the latest clothes. Where have you been lately?"

"Not in London. Can't you tell?"

We turn in through a swing door into the darkest, blackest shop I could ever imagine. It's like entering Santa's Grotto, but with fewer fairy lights. How anyone could hope to see the dresses hanging here is beyond me, let alone examine any price tags. Which are also no doubt, beyond my meagre spending capacity.

"But I can't see," I wail.

"Shut up," hisses Alison. "You'll get us thrown out."

"Good. Come on, Jill. Let's stand by the door so at least we can see daylight."

Crossing the road at night at Piccadilly Circus is an education. The name alone conveys to me mayhem, as in the phrase when everything is chaotic, 'It's like Piccadilly Circus in here'. And indeed, that is what I can see before me. At half past ten in the evening, traffic is flowing as freely as if it is Monday morning rush hour. As we stand on an island in the middle of the road, neon lights flashing on all sides, it looks impossible to cross, with no gap in the constant flow of cars and taxis. I gaze around, overwhelmed by the noise of the traffic and blare of horns, such as I have never experienced before.

I declare dramatically, "So, this is Piccadilly Circus!"

Alison and Caroline have to grab an arm each and propel me across the road behind the others before we are mown down by a black cab.

The journey back on the coach feels like a nightmare. By now, we are suffering from the full effects of being deprived of sleep. To make matters worse, the coach gets a puncture and we wait more than an hour in a layby while the driver walks to an AA phone box to summon help.

In the grey light of morning, without having slept a wink, the four of our little group who live in Beechwood House bid farewell to Helen and Catherine and drag ourselves along the path, willing our feet to keep moving. In just over twenty-four hours, we have travelled hundreds of miles and toured six landmarks of the capital. Our faces are ashen and our limbs feel like lead.

"Never again," Alison moans. "My feet are killing me."

"I think we must have seen more of London in one day than some folk see in a whole week," I say, trying to sound positive. "Managing to fit in a show as well must be a record."

"Do you know, I can't remember much about that," says Jill, yawning. "I think I must have slept through it."

The main doors of Beechwood swing shut behind us, echoing up the silent corridor. Alison goes straight to her room, flings her handbag across the floor and drops like a straight log onto her bed. Brenda disappears into her own domain, while Jill heads to the kitchen to switch the kettle on. I lean against the wall in Alison's room, take off my shoes and rub the bruised soles of my feet.

"That's been a hard way to learn where the Fire of London started."

"Where?" mumbles Alison into her pillow.

"It was Pudding Lane."

"I didn't see that. When did we go there?"

"On the way to the Victoria and Albert. What's the use of going to London if you don't learn something?"

"Well, I've learned that the next time I'm staying overnight in a nice hotel," says Jill, bringing in the coffees and a mug of her usual strong tea.

Revived by the hot drink, Alison recovers enough to demand we examine each other's purchases. We duly empty our bags and pass round for inspection a light blue jumper in pure lambswool, a visitor's guide to the Victoria and Albert and a notebook and matching pencil emblazoned with red double decker buses.

"And I bought something to wear for the Summer Ball," I announce.

Alison is fully awake now and wonders how I could afford such a thing. Jill brings up the subject of partners and says she isn't sure how we can even think about attending the Ball without them.

"You can't just turn up with no one to dance with. And none of us has anyone lined up."

"Have you not heard the latest?" says Alison. "Brenda has some hare-brained scheme about ringing up the local RAF camp and getting them to send a few men over."

Jill nearly splutters on her tea. "Do you think they'll really do that? Anyway, I doubt they'd come up to Amelia's exacting standards. Servicemen don't normally wear elbow patches on corduroy jackets."

Being quite used to the constant teasing about this and aware that my criteria are wholly unreasonable, I ignore her remark. "Do you want to see it, then?"

I hold up my newly acquired long-length ball dress, a delicate creation in white cotton. It has narrow pink stripes of ribbon running through it, short puffy sleeves, a low scooped neckline and a gathered bodice. A character in a Jane Austen novel would be proud to wear it. Alison and Jill murmur their approval.

"Go on then," they urge. "How expensive was it?"

I smile innocently. "Not expensive at all, because I didn't buy it in the evening wear section. And I definitely didn't get in Biba's. I could afford it because, it's a *nightie* from Marks and Spencer's."

CHAPTER THIRTY-SEVEN

~~~

JUNE AND JULY 1972

THE END OF THE ROAD

"Amelia, don't you wish you had that finished?"

Helen looks at me anxiously. I'm sitting bolt upright at my desk, my fingers pounding the typewriter keys, occasionally pushing hair out of my eyes to squint at a word written carelessly in my notes. I am vaguely aware of the sounds of chatter and the occasional burst of laughter from outside. The others are larking about on the lawn in the sunshine outside my window: their work done, 'Main Subject Special Studies' complete.

"I'm almost at the end of this last chapter. And then there's only the conclusion and that's already in my notebook in rough," I breathe between tapping the shift key and then the space bar. The origins of the character of Heathcliff in *Wuthering Heights*, my all-time favourite novel, have consumed both my waking thoughts and my dreams for months. I tell her she should be out there with them, enjoying our last few weeks of freedom.

Helen leans back in my easy chair next to the bookcase and runs her fingers along the many volumes that have become like old friends: *The Psychology of Play, The Development of Language* and *Piaget's Theories*. She picks out the thickest book, with the scintillating title of *The Plowden Report*. For three years this has been our Education Bible, with its message that the child lies at the heart of it all. No longer must teachers slavishly push their pupils through the Eleven Plus, with their classes in rows facing the blackboard, chanting their multiplication tables. Creativity was not allowed, but this is a new era and we are part of it.

She idly flicks the well-thumbed pages and puts it back. "I don't mind keeping you company. It's not a nice feeling, working on your own with everyone else finished."

I notice her freckles are more pronounced after a few days of June sunshine.

She pauses and shakes her head. "I can't believe we'll all be gone this time next month."

"Not unless some of us get externals," I say, keeping my eyes on the fast-emerging words on the white paper.

I reach the bottom of the page. "Damnation!"

I begin feverishly looking for my little bottle of

correction fluid. Helen reaches across, moves a file to one side and hands me the white liquid saviour.

"Thanks. You'd make someone a good secretary."

In two seconds, the offending letter is painted out.

"How about a good headmistress?" she asks.

I screw the lid back on the miniature bottle and look at her properly. "Is that what you want to do? All I can envisage is a classroom with thirty children and me in the middle, trying to engage their little minds." I sigh. "And sometimes even that vision evades me."

I wind another new sheet of paper into the typewriter.

"No, being serious, Helen. I can see you as a headmistress. I think you'd make a good one. You'd have the school running in perfect order."

We smile at each other and I resume my frantic typing.

The final fortnight is upon us. Special Studies for Education and Main Subject, each containing thousands of words are complete. The Summer Ball is behind us.

Courtesy of Brenda's daring phone call, RAF Winston sent over six officers who duly escorted us from Beechwood House across to the main hall in College, and I wore my Jane Austen cotton nightie-cum-dress. The experience brought back memories of my dates with unfortunate Keith in the first year. A total stranger is not for me. I have decided I need a friend first: a best friend who turns into a partner for life, a soul-mate, whatever label one might like to choose.

Along with Alison, Jill and Brenda and occasionally Helen, Becky and Catherine, we fully immerse ourselves in our last few days. We borrow bicycles one balmy evening to ride up and down the College paths; we lie on the grassy banks to watch cricket matches, clapping sporadically along with the other lazy spectators; we talk and talk, lounging around my room until three in the morning until the sky lightens in an early dawn before succumbing to a few hours of exhausted sleep.

The last fateful list goes up on the notice board and we hurry over to read the names of those who have been chosen to suffer an external examiner. The small print tells us that all the named students are randomly chosen, which cheers us slightly.

Helen, Catherine and I are on the list. The others must go down without us.

It's Wednesday and two days before the official end of term and end of year. Every time Alison catches sight of Helen she dissolves into tears, declaring she will never see her again.

"Of course you will," Helen laughs, while she pats her on the back in a reassuring way. "You're coming up to stay with me in August, remember?"

"But things won't ever be the same," Alison wails. Then she sniffs and blows her nose.

Although the rest of us scoff at her melodramatics, we

are all feeling the same, but we try to hide it. I know she's right. Things won't ever be the same again.

Now it's Friday. We've had high tea in the dining room and made banana sandwiches for the last time, scraped our plastic trays on the way out, put our sheets outside the door for our laundry, drunk our last cup of coffee and dunked the last digestive in the packet.

Catherine has brought her overflowing carrier bag to leave in my room, but it's not laundry. This time she's staying in Jill's room to keep me company for our two extra nights, when we must stay behind for the externals. Alison, Brenda and Jill have packed their cases and are ready to wend their way down into town for the bus.

Catherine and I stand at my open window to wave. The little group moves further and further away along the path. After every two or three steps, Alison sets her cases on the ground to turn and cry out, "But I don't want to go", whereupon we laugh and shout, "Hurry up, you'll miss the bus". We have to be a little heartless, as otherwise Alison will never leave. They reach the end of the path, pass through the White Gates and our friends at last disappear out of sight.

Lying alone in my single bed, the curtains closed against the summer night and Beechwood House eerily half-empty and bereft, the echoes of my long-ago, painful interview resound in my mind.

More than three years and it feels as if I have lived a whole lifetime since. Wanting to open up the wonders of the world to young children had been my desire. I have travelled far, and my destination is almost in sight. I have pulled out every ounce of courage within me, but I know even more will be required. A school and a classroom with real live children await me.

And what of my search for the person who will allow me to be truly myself? No one ever came up, metaphorically, to tap me on the shoulder and say, 'Oh, it's you at last', or 'Where have you been hiding?' and I have decided not to accept any less. I have never seen what I have wanted to see in any of the faces I have beheld.

Once I said to Judith, "If I leave College without finding him, I shall buy a sports car and go on every extra teaching course I can."

Her reply? "Well then, you won't be single for long."

I think I shall have to start saving.

As we drive away in Pete's car, the boot packed with books and belongings, I turn round in the passenger seat for one last look. I whisper goodbye to Beechwood, Number 3 Northgate and Dale House. Overlooking the wide lawns and majestic trees, St Mag's College stands proudly, soon to be empty and silent, waiting to receive another intake of new students. Perhaps some of them will be as wide-eyed and eager as I was: ready for new friendships, new experiences and one of the best adventures in their lives.

Today, I'm going home, back to the North East, to become Miss Hardy with a class of my own.

POSTSCRIPT

~~~~

JULY 22ND AND 23RD 1972

WHEN THE RAIN STOPS

"Put my name down for the last dance," he says, in a matter-of-fact tone. "It's Jon without an 'h', Jon Trevanian."

I scribble his name at the bottom of the little card I've been given.

"That's Cornish," he points out. "My family came up from Cornwall. Well, not just last week. Generations ago. Walked up to the North East with everything piled on a cart."

He smiles a big wide smile. I like that. He talks a lot. I like that as well.

"Righto, Jon without the 'h'. See you tonight at the dance."

I give him, I hope, an equally friendly smile and put my filled-up dance card in the back pocket of my new herringbone trousers. At first I thought this was an old-fashioned idea, to decide who you're going to partner beforehand, but I've been assured it's a great way of getting to know everyone and it always takes place here on the first night.

We're up in Scotland, at St Andrews University to be exact. There'd been one last place on the Church Youth Annual Holiday: a study week cum holiday, actually. Debates and talks every morning and afternoons free. Non-obligatory evening services thrown in. I've just come from College and now it looks as though I'm going back. Except, rather than studying Education, I'm assured we will be looking at 'the meaning of life' and other interesting topics. Now that would be more than beneficial. It's always good to understand the meaning of life, as I'm still looking for it.

It was only last week when the Curate called in for coffee at Mam's house. It seems her whole adult life has been dedicated to entertaining vicars and curates. During the course of the conversation, while I carried out my old role of handing round the tea plates, the stout, rosy-faced man of the cloth happened to say, "Someone's dropped out of this year's church trip." Just before taking another large mouthful of homemade Victoria jam sponge, he added, looking directly at me, "Do you fancy taking the last place?"

Mam and I glanced at each other. Could we afford it? That was more like the real question. It's true I needed some kind of diversion, as College seemed a long time ago and teaching wouldn't start until September.

Once we'd waved The Reverend off from the front door, we set to on the task of scraping together the eighteen pounds I needed, even raiding all the money boxes lying around the house. In the end I managed to pay for the week away with an extra £5 note and a pound in change to put in my purse for spending money. Not much, but I reckon I can just about cope, if I'm not too lavish. I've spent the last three years being frugal, so one week should be easy.

This morning I sat on the back seat of the bus ready for the long journey up to Scotland. The other girls, including the Vicar's daughter, Laura, who is the only one I really know, were in a state of excitement. As the coach stopped to pick up more passengers for our St Andrews holiday, Laura nudged me with her elbow.

"Here's Jon!" They already knew him from last year.

I turned around in my seat and just caught a glimpse of him stowing away his luggage in the boot of the coach, while his dad, or the man I assumed to be his dad, handed him what looked like a fishing rod.

As Jon came on board, everyone greeted him like a long-lost friend. I was the new girl, sitting in the middle of the back seat, the one person on the bus he didn't know. He sat just in front of us and I was happy to listen to the friendly chatter between him and the other girls. I saw him again briefly at our evening meal tonight, but all we could do was smile and wave to each other across the long table.

Now, it's the 'getting to know each other' dance. Every time the song changes, we girls must find the boy whose name is the next one written on our dance card. For a few manic moments, I roam around the crowd of young people, calling out, "Steven, where are you?" I've met and danced with each boy and had a two-minute, limited conversation as we tried to hear one another above the disco music.

This is the last song and there's only Jon to find. Although not as tall as the others, he's easy to spot, as he gives me another of his wide smiles and I notice it shows in his eyes.

As I might have predicted, the last dance is of course a slow one: a bit awkward when you could find yourself nose to nose with someone you've just met, or in my case, it would be nose to chest, my nose to his chest. Just awkward.

"Would you like a walk out?" I hear him ask, cutting through the plaintive strains of Don McLean's 'Vincent'. "I want to have a look at the petrol pumps at the garage down the road."

This is a strange suggestion. It sounds suspiciously like a variation on 'nipping behind the bike shed'.

I have to ask. "Why the petrol pumps?"

"Well, they're all going to go self-service soon and I want to read the instructions," Jon explains.

Although it still sounds like a novel idea just to get me out of the dance hall and outside, I decide to take the chance. His face shows a genuine demeanour that makes me feel safe, and there's something about the arch of his eyebrows and the way his long light brown hair brushes against the collar of his black shirt.

And so we leave the flashing lights, the warmth of the hall and the closely dancing bodies moving side to side as the evocative song reaches the starry, starry night chorus. Without a backward glance, we step out into the cold, dark evening.

We don't look up into the sky to search for stars, nor look for them in each other's eyes. Instead, now that we can actually hear each other speak, Jon keeps up a non-stop chatter all the way to the garage. He is curious about my time at College and how that is a goal he aspires to himself. When I suggest giving it a try, he explains how he already has a plan. And what does he do in his spare time, I ask? He chuckles and tells me that as a qualified motor mechanic, he spends most weekends underneath his dad's car, fixing it. It seems there is nothing Jon doesn't know about the workings of an engine.

True to his word, when we reach the garage, which is closed and devoid of any sign of life, he inspects the petrol pumps and reads every word of the instructions.

And then we stroll back to the university. We talk all the way, and I like that. Our goodnight is simply a friendly wave and a 'see you at breakfast' sort of promise. And I like that too.

It's Sunday: a free day for us to explore this university town. Dressed in my best flowery blouse and denim jeans, ready for the promise of fine weather, I join Laura's table in the dining hall. There's the alluring smell of fried bacon and hot toast. It feels much more like being on holiday than being at College.

By the time we are draining our coffee cups, some of the girls have decided to go down to the harbour and hire a rowing boat. Jon, sitting opposite me and a little further down the long table, offers to come along. So far, he's been in animated conversation with a girl next to him and has only given me a few glances, albeit friendly ones. Laura seems keen for him to join our venture, as she is quick to point out that he would be handy, having broad shoulders to take the oars.

The sun shines, the water sparkles and we are all full of laughter and good humour while Jon obligingly rows up and down negotiating the swell of the sea and I keep one hand on my cream straw sunhat as the breeze whips up over the water.

Our time is up and we step out of the rocking boat onto dry land, with gallant assistance from our reliable rower. Laura suggests heading into town, but Jon offers to show me the castle, which I'd much rather see, so we part company with the rest of the group.

He takes me on a historical tour, describing all the battles enacted long ago among the ruins, while he leaps off crumbling walls, brandishes an imaginary sword and explains the finer points of weaponry. I listen and nod and laugh and am altogether enjoying myself. I tell him about the class of children waiting for me to be their teacher in September. He expands about his own similar ambitions: to leave his cold, draughty garage for a life in front of the blackboard, once he is qualified.

I forget the unreasonable superficial criteria I used to hold dear: the jacket with the patched sleeves and the piano playing. He fits neither of these. But I don't care. He's funny and kind and I never once have to wonder what to say next. I realise that this has been my most important criterion all along. Perhaps when we were children, we met by chance on the beach and played together on the sand, where I know he would have lent me his spade. It could quite easily have happened. If it didn't, it should have.

With the tour over, just as we step back through the castle gates out onto the street, the first big drops of rain start: randomly onto the dry ground initially and then heavier and more constant.

Jon and I are running now. My straw hat droops and he laughs and carries it for me. We see a café and rush for the door. The bell gives a welcome jingle as we dash into the warmth and the noisy chatter and then we stand, dripping onto the entrance mat. Looking around, I see with dismay that all of the tables are full of couples and families, talking and clattering tea cups and saucers. But we find the last two empty chairs at the end of a long table and as the customers shuffle up to give us more room, they look with a smile on their faces at our wet hair and rosy cheeks. As I sip my hot tea I don't mind that my hat has died in the rain and my damp blouse is clinging to my arms.

I look over the top of my china cup at Jon, sitting opposite. As he looks back at me, I am certain that he knows too.

The rain outside clears and I pick up my now useless sunhat. We close the café door behind us, begin a slow walk back along the shiny pavements and hold hands.

AFTERWORD

~~~

2019

In June 2019, St Margaret's validating University came to the decision to confer honorary degrees upon their students who held Certificates in Education. In an official letter, it stated that this was to recognise the rigours of the teacher training course we had undergone for three years and for our services given to children and their education. We could now add to our names the letters BA, Bachelor of Art (honoris causa).

We wore gowns and hoods and mortar boards and had our photographs taken to be framed and hung upon our walls at home. Afternoon tea was served in a huge marquee. That special day was the sweetness of all icing on our lightest of all cakes.

In September 2019, we held a reunion: a celebration marking fifty years since our arrival in 1969 at St Margaret's Church of England College of Education as nervous, excited students. Seated around a long, dining table, I looked at the still familiar faces, Alison, Jill, Catherine and Becky among them. We talked while we ate, and laughed while we indulged in reminiscing. Our friendship has remained steadfast. Whenever we are together, we are still those eighteen-year olds, full of girlish glee and fun. St Mag's is still a part of us all and no one can deny us our shared, fond memories.

True to the spirit of College, the sun shone and all was well with the world.

But where was Helen? Serious, conscientious Helen, who we all expected to become a career woman, an inspirational headmistress? We raised a glass in her memory, to a life cut short in her twenties. We will never forget the girl from Cumbria.

And what of Amelia Hardy?

It was September 1974, the first day of the new term, only two years after becoming 'Miss Hardy' the teacher, when I stood in front of another new class. I opened the register and looked at the thirty expectant faces before me. As I called their names, it was music to my ears to hear each child reply not 'Yes Miss Hardy', but instead, 'Yes Mrs Trevanian'.

Printed in Great Britain
by Amazon

54269494R00180